Number and calculations 4

Series Editor: Tony Cotton

Series Consultant: Ian Thompson

Pearson Education
Edinburgh Gate
Harlow
Essex
CM20 2JE

Series Editor: Tony Cotton
Series Consultant: Ian Thompson

Contributors to Year 4 Number and calculations Pupils' Book:
Graham Astley, Anne Barber, Alison Borthwick, Alison Brunt, Paula Ann Coombes, Maria Curry, Colin Penfold and
Allison Toogood.

The authors and publishers would like to thank all the schools that trialled lessons for Longman MathsWorks.

ISBN 0582 81888 5

ACKNOWLEDGEMENTS

We are grateful to the following for permission to reproduce copyright photographs:
Alamy Images for page 122 bottom middle; Alamy Images/Comstock for page 119 top; Corbis for page 61 bottom;
DK Images for pages 42 middle right, 122 top, 122 bottom left, 122 middle left, 122 middle right, 122 bottom right,
122 middle centre; DK Images/British Museum for pages 42 top, 42 left, 42 right, 42 bottom, 42 middle left;
Image Source for page 104; Punchstock/PhotoDisc for page 123.

The following photographs were taken on commission by Chris Fairclough:
pages 5, 6, 7, 8, 10, 21, 22, 28, 29, 30, 47, 48, 61 top, 65, 66, 77, 78, 82, 83, 84, 97, 118, 119 bottom, 121,124, 125, 126.

Cover photo: W. Cody/Corbis

Picture research by Hilary Luckcock

Illustrated by Emma Brownjohn (New Division), Craig Cameron (Art Collection), Edmond Davis (Meiklejohn) and
Melanie Sharp (Sylvie Poggio).

Printed in China
GCC/01

Abbreviations and symbols

⚠ core work

◎ support work

▣ extension work

➤ lesson continued over page

▦ use a calculator

Contents

Place value, ordering and rounding 1

You can use different strategies to estimate about how many or about how much.

⚠ Estimate quantities

> What fraction of the jars are full?

1 When they are full, these jars hold about 60 biscuits. Estimate how many biscuits there are in each jar.

2 Repeat **question 1**, for jars that hold 30 biscuits.

You will need RS 1.

3 Estimate how many children are:
   a playing football
   b practising netball
   c skipping
   d in the field
   e on the climbing frame
   f in the playground.

4 There are about 200 children at school today.
   a Estimate how many are playing outside.
   b The rest are having lunch. Estimate how many are having lunch.

> You can use grouping to help you estimate.
>
>   x x x
> x x x x x
> x x x x x
> x x   x
>
> There are roughly 3 rows and 5 columns. 3 × 5 = 15

➤ Place value, ordering and rounding 1

You can use different strategies to estimate about how many or about how much.

@ How many pennies?

You will need:
- a partner
- a pile of about 100 pennies
- small transparent pots.

1   Each pick up a handful of pennies. Spread them out without letting any overlap. Estimate the number of pennies. Check your partner's estimate by moving the pennies into rows of five.

2   Repeat with two handfuls of pennies and three handfuls of pennies.

3   Take turns to fill the pots with pennies and estimate how many pennies each one holds. Check your partner's estimate by counting. Stack the pennies into piles of ten to check. Use your results to improve your estimates.

4   Estimate first and then check how many:
  a pennies cover the bottom of the pot
  b layers of pennies fill the container
  c pennies make the container half full.

➤ Place value, ordering and rounding 1

You can use different strategies to estimate about how many or about how much.

▣ Estimating numbers

You will need:
- a partner
- RS 1
- some skipping ropes
- some string
- a metre rule.

1 a Look at this picture. Estimate how many children are queuing for lunch.
  b Look at the plan on RS 1. There are about 200 children at the school.
    At lunchtime most children are playing outside.
    The rest are eating in the hall or queuing for lunch.
    About how many children are playing outside?
  c Estimate how many children are in the hall eating their lunch.

2 Your skipping ropes are too long!
  a Estimate what fraction of each rope you would have to cut off to make it 1 m long.
    Do not cut the rope!
  b   Cut a piece of string to match the length of the fraction.
                                       Check your estimate by finding how many
                                       times you can fit your piece of string along
                                       the whole length of the rope.

You can use rounding to help you place a number on a number line.

⚠ Rounding and comparing

You will need:
- plain paper
- a ruler
- a dice.

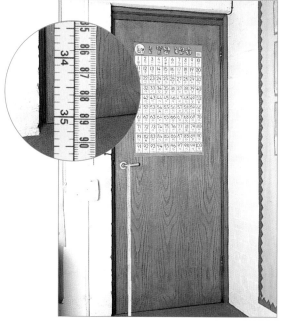

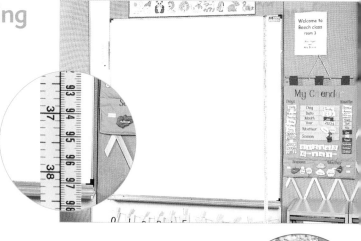

1   Round the measurements on the measuring tapes above to the nearest 10 cm.

2   Round the measurements on the measuring tapes below to the nearest 1 cm.

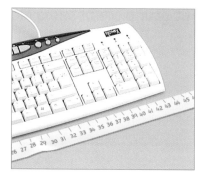

➤ Place value, ordering and rounding 2

You can use rounding to help you place a number on a number line.

3 a Roll the dice four times.
   b Use the digits to make two 2-digit numbers.
   c Round each number to the nearest 10.
   d Draw a number line. Label the ends and the
      halfway mark.

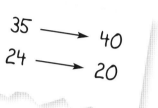

   e Mark on all the numbers that you make as accurately
      as you can.

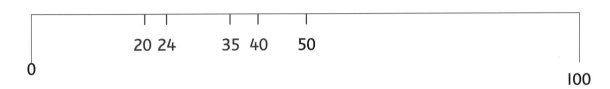

   f Write a number that lies between each pair of numbers on the line.
   g Use any of your numbers and the symbols < or > to write four number sentences.
      e.g.

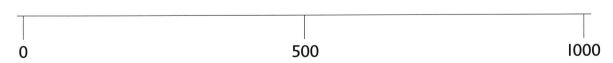

4 a Roll the dice 6 times to make two 3-digit numbers.
   b Round your numbers to the nearest 10 first and then the nearest 100.
   c Mark your numbers on a 0 – 1000 number line.

```
|——————————————————|——————————————————|
0                  500                 1000
```

➤ Place value, ordering and rounding 2

You can use rounding to help you place a number on a number line.

🔁 Rounding and comparing numbers and measurements

You will need:
- a partner
- a metre rule
- three 0 – 9 dice
- coloured pens
- a roll of paper.

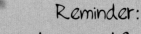

Reminder:
1 cm = 10 mm
10 cm = 100 mm

1   Use the metre rule to draw a line that is 1 m
    long on a strip of paper. Roll the dice three times
    so that you have three different numbers.

2   Arrange the numbers on the dice in different ways to
    make six 3-digit lengths in millimetres, e.g. 253 mm.
    For each number:
    a find the number on the metre rule and
       round it to the nearest 100 mm
    b mark the rounded number under the line
    c round it to the nearest 10 mm, recording it under the line
    d mark its position as accurately as you can without using the metre rule
    e check your estimated position by measuring and mark the actual position
       in a different colour.

3   Write six number statements using the numbers that you made and the symbols < and >,
    e.g. 253 < 532.

Challenge
Record the error in your estimated position in a number sentence:
estimated position = actual position +/− error

Place value, ordering and rounding 4

You can round numbers to find a rough answer or estimate.

⚠ Checking using rounding

This calculator works out addition, subtraction and multiplication calculations.
Today it is getting some calculations wrong.

1   Use rounding to work out which calculations look wrong.
    Explain your answers.

    a   `142+179=521`   b   `23×4=72`

    c   `252+145=397`   d   `506-460=146`

    e   `895-216=679`   f   `17×11=257`

2   Use rounding to work out approximate answers to these.

    a   `355-204`   b   `59÷49`

    c   `19×5`   d   `27×6`

    e   `932÷123`   f   `768-197`

3   Choose one of the calculations in **question 2**. Write a word problem for this
    calculation where an approximate answer would be all that is needed,
    e.g. There were 355 burgers. 204 were eaten. About how many were left?

➤ Place value, ordering and rounding 4

You can round numbers to find a rough answer or estimate.

◎ Rounding to the nearest 10

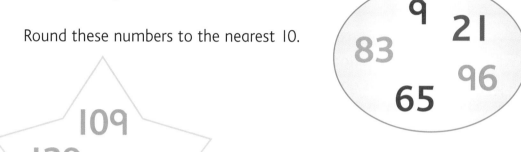

1   Round these numbers to the nearest 10.

109
139   221
507   48

2   Round the numbers in the star to the nearest 100.

3   Class 4 is doing a school play.

Round the numbers
to the nearest 10 to
find an estimate.

Use your answers from **question 1** to help you answer the following.
a   They sell 83 tickets for the first day and 96 tickets for the second day.
    About how many tickets have they sold altogether?
b   There are nine rows of chairs with 21 in each row.
    Estimate the total number of chairs. Are there enough?
c   Make up your own problem about the play and estimate the answer.

You can multiply a number by 10 by moving the digits one place to the left. Divide by 10 by moving one place to the right.

▣ Times 10 again

1   Write a single digit in the middle of a page.

2   Multiply this number by 10 and write this number above the first number. Repeat, working up the page, until you have five numbers.

3   a   Now divide your original number by 10. Write the new number below your original number.

    b   Repeat, working down the page. What patterns can you see?

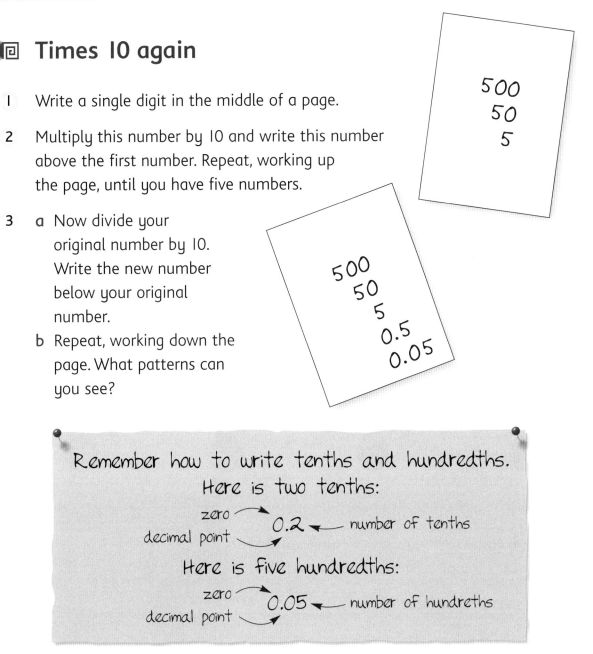

Remember how to write tenths and hundredths.

Here is two tenths:

zero → 0.2 ← number of tenths
decimal point →

Here is five hundredths:

zero → 0.05 ← number of hundreths
decimal point →

Challenge

What happens when you divide a whole number with up to four digits by 10 and then multiply the answer by 100?

You can use negative numbers to describe temperatures lower than 0°C.

⚠ Find the temperature

You will need RS 9.

1
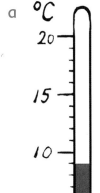

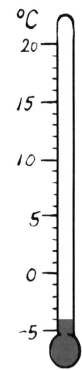

Look at the thermometers. Write each temperature.

2   The next day all the temperatures in **question 1** are 1°C lower. Show the new temperatures on RS 9.

3   Show these temperatures on RS 9.
     a −3°C
     b 8°C

4   The temperatures in **question 3** rise by 2°C. Write the new temperatures.

You can use negative numbers to describe temperatures lower than 0°C.

◎ What's the temperature?

1   Write the temperature for each thermometer.

a   °C

b   °C
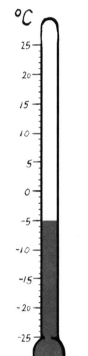

c   °C

d   °C

You need RS 9.

2   Make each thermometer show one of these temperatures.
   a 5°C
   b −1°C
   c −5°C
   d 10°C
   e −2°C
   f 1°C

You can use negative numbers to describe temperatures lower than 0°C.

🔁 Temperature tricks

You will need:
- a group of three players
- a set of temperature cards from −10°C to 10°C.

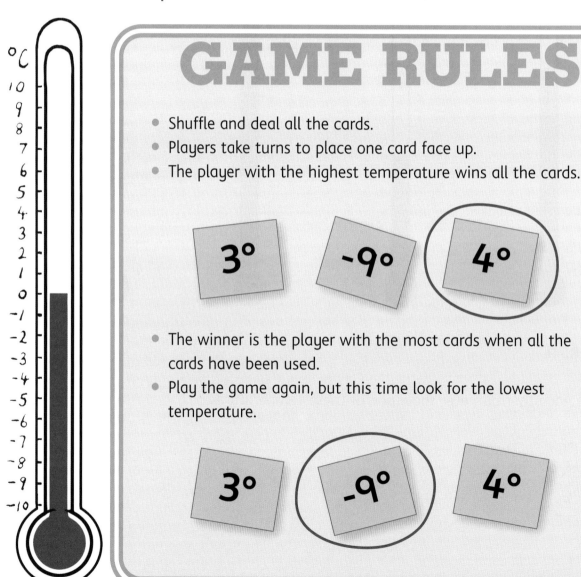

GAME RULES

- Shuffle and deal all the cards.
- Players take turns to place one card face up.
- The player with the highest temperature wins all the cards.

3° -9° 4°

- The winner is the player with the most cards when all the cards have been used.
- Play the game again, but this time look for the lowest temperature.

3° -9° 4°

°C
10
9
8
7
6
5
4
3
2
1
0
−1
−2
−3
−4
−5
−6
−7
−8
−9
−10

You can work out the rule for number sequences and use this to complete them more quickly.

⚠ Complete the sequence

1   Complete this sequence: __, __, 17, __, 31, __

Here is one way to do it. Draw a number line. Put a box for each number and draw the jumps between each box. Fill in the numbers you know.

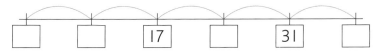

Find the difference between the two numbers given.

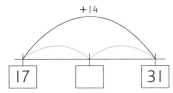

Split into equal jumps.

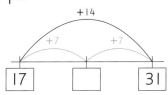

> Remember the jump between each number is of equal size each time.

You need to count how many jumps there are between the two numbers.

The rule is +7.

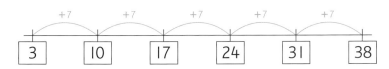

2   Copy and complete these number sequences.

a   __, 14, __, 24, __, __

b   __, __, 26, __, 44, __

c   __, 11, __, 27, __, __

d   __, 21, __, 45, __, __

e   __, __, 34, __, 64, __

f   __, 24, __, __, 42, __

Properties of numbers and number sequences 3

You can make number sequences that have negative numbers in them.

⚠ Go negative

You will need:
- a dice with numbers 1 – 6
- cards with numbers 1 – 10.

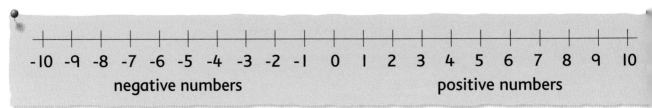

negative numbers   positive numbers

You will be creating number sequences with seven numbers.

Roll the dice to get the size of each step.

Pick a card to get the starting number.

The starting number is always the 4th number in the sequence.

I rolled the dice. The step size is 4.
I picked a card. The 4th number is 9.

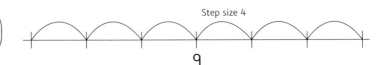

Step size 4

9

You might find it helpful to mark zero to remind you when you move into negative numbers.

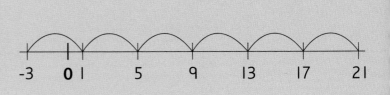

-3   0 1   5   9   13   17   21

Create your own sequences of seven numbers.

You can make number sequences that have negative numbers in them.

▣ Negative or positive

You will need:

- cards with numbers 1 – 20
- cards with numbers 10 – 20.

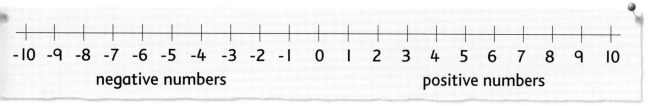

-10 -9 -8 -7 -6 -5 -4 -3 -2 -1 0 1 2 3 4 5 6 7 8 9 10

negative numbers   positive numbers

You will be creating number sequences with seven numbers.

Pick a card between 1 and 20 to get the size of steps.
Pick a card between 10 and 20 to get the starting number.
The starting number is always the 4th number in the sequence.

> I picked a card. The step size is 12.
> I picked a card. The 4th number is 18.

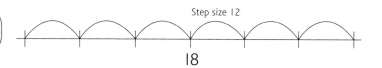

Step size 12

18

You might find it helpful to mark zero to remind you when you move into negative numbers.

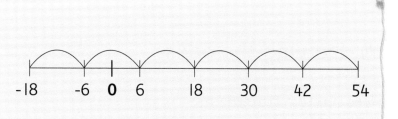

-18   -6   **0**   6   18   30   42   54

Create your own sequences of seven numbers.

You can give examples to show that a statement about odd and even numbers is false.

⚠ Odd or even?

Here are two statements:
- **Odd + odd + even = even.**
- **Even − odd = even.**

Make up five calculations that show whether these statements are true.
Use numbers less than 100. Try to explain why each statement is true or false.

◎ How odd

Here are two statements:
- **Odd numbers can never be in the 2 times table.**
- **The sum of two odd numbers is always odd.**

Use numbers below 20 to show whether you think each statement is true. Find five examples for each statement.

▣ Halving the odds

Here are two statements:
- **Odd numbers cannot be halved.**
- **The product of two even numbers is always odd.**

Find some examples to show whether each statement is always true, sometimes true or never true. Find five examples for each statement. Try to explain what you find out.

You can recognise multiples of 2, 3, 4, 5 and 10.

⚠ Multiple riddles

1 Mrs Jervis needs four teams of children to practise netball skills. There are 30 children in the netball club. How could she organise the children in teams so that there are an equal number of children playing against each other in a game?

> There doesn't have to be seven on each team.

2 Mike organises his 20 stamps in his album. He could stick five on a page and there would be three pages left blank. He could stick four on a page and there would be two pages left blank.

  a How many pages are there in the album?
  b How else could he organise the stamps?

3 Investigate different ways to organise:
  a 40 stickers in an album that has got 7 pages
  b 30 photos in an album that has got 9 pages
  c 50 pictures in a scrapbook that has 11 pages.

4 Talya counts her teddy bears in groups of five. She has four left over. She counts her bears in groups of four. She has two left over.
  a Investigate how many bears Talya might have.
  b Work out three different ways that she could organise the bears in equal groups.

You can recognise multiples of 2, 3, 4, 5 and 10.

◎ What's left over?

1   David counts his toy cars in threes. There are two left over. He counts his cars in fives. There is one left over. How many cars could David have?

2   Investigate different ways to organise:
    a   19 stickers on three pages
    b   24 stamps on five pages
    c   30 pictures on four pages.

3   Use 37 coins or cubes. Work out how many are left over if you count them in:
    a   twos   b   threes   c   fours
    d   fives   e   tens.

▣ Division riddles

1   There are 50 bean bags in the PE cupboard. Investigate different ways to share them out in a class of 30 children that are organised in:
    a   five groups   b   six groups.

2   Tim has a jar of 20p coins. He counts them in groups of five. He has two left over. He counts them in groups of ten. He has seven left over.
    a   How many 20p coins could Tim have?
    b   How much money is this?
    c   How could he count them in equal groups?

3   Write division riddles similar to **question 2** for your friends to investigate.

You can use a fraction to show part of a whole.

⚠ Note the fraction

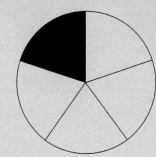

To recognise a fraction you need to know how many equal parts make a whole.

This shape is split into 5 equal parts.
1 part is shaded.
We call this one fifth or $\frac{1}{5}$.

1   Are these shapes split equally?

a
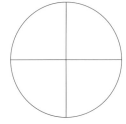

b

c

d
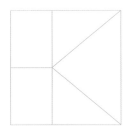

e
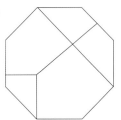

f

g
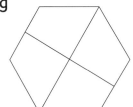

h

You can use a fraction to show part of a whole.

2   Write down the fraction of each shape that is shaded.

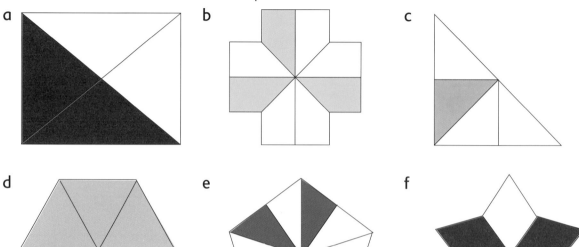

a   b   c

d   e   f

3   Write down the fraction of each shape that is not shaded.

Challenge
Work through RS 22.

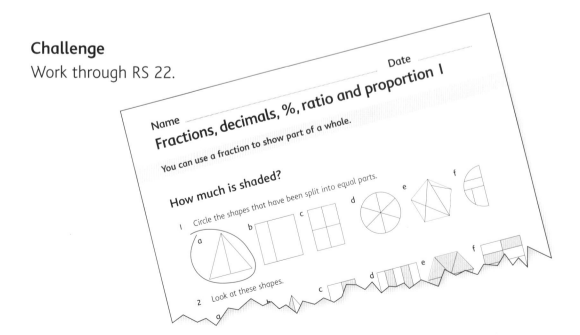

Name
Date
Fractions, decimals, %, ratio and proportion I
You can use a fraction to show part of a whole.

How much is shaded?

I   Circle the shapes that have been split into equal parts.
a   b   c   d   e   f

2   Look at these shapes.
a   b   c   d   e   f

You can use a fraction to show part of a whole.

▣ Fraction partners

1 Look at the shapes.
Write down the fraction
of each shape that is shaded.

> To recognise a fraction you need to know how many equal parts are in a whole.

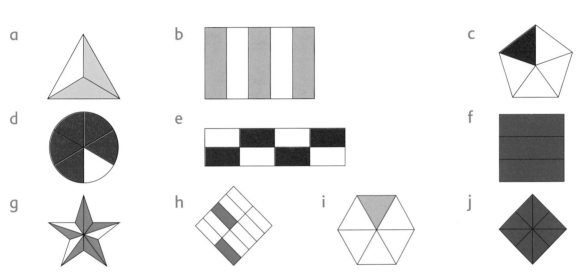

a   b   c

d   e   f

g   h   i   j

2 Write down the fraction of each shape that is not shaded.

3 These fractions need a partner to make 1 whole.
Write each fraction in your book.
Decide what fraction they need to make 1.

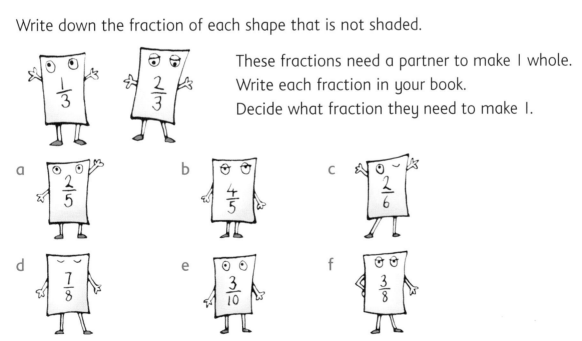

$\frac{1}{3}$ $\frac{2}{3}$

a $\frac{2}{5}$ b $\frac{4}{5}$ c $\frac{2}{6}$

d $\frac{7}{8}$ e $\frac{3}{10}$ f $\frac{3}{8}$

Fractions, decimals, %, ratio and proportion 2

You can say whether a fraction is bigger or smaller than a half.

⚠ ▣ Are they equal?

1									
$\frac{1}{2}$					$\frac{1}{2}$				
$\frac{1}{3}$			$\frac{1}{3}$			$\frac{1}{3}$			
$\frac{1}{4}$		$\frac{1}{4}$		$\frac{1}{4}$			$\frac{1}{4}$		
$\frac{1}{5}$		$\frac{1}{5}$		$\frac{1}{5}$		$\frac{1}{5}$		$\frac{1}{5}$	
$\frac{1}{6}$		$\frac{1}{6}$		$\frac{1}{6}$		$\frac{1}{6}$		$\frac{1}{6}$	$\frac{1}{6}$
$\frac{1}{8}$	$\frac{1}{8}$	$\frac{1}{8}$	$\frac{1}{8}$	$\frac{1}{8}$	$\frac{1}{8}$	$\frac{1}{8}$	$\frac{1}{8}$		
$\frac{1}{10}$	$\frac{1}{10}$	$\frac{1}{10}$	$\frac{1}{10}$	$\frac{1}{10}$	$\frac{1}{10}$	$\frac{1}{10}$	$\frac{1}{10}$	$\frac{1}{10}$	$\frac{1}{10}$

Use the fraction wall to answer these questions.

1   Write down the fractions that are equal to:

     a $\frac{1}{2}$ b $\frac{1}{4}$ c $\frac{3}{4}$ d $\frac{1}{3}$ e $\frac{1}{5}$

     f $\frac{6}{8}$ g $\frac{2}{3}$ h $\frac{8}{10}$ i $\frac{2}{5}$ j $\frac{3}{5}$.

> Some fractions are equal to one whole.
> For example: $\frac{2}{2}$ = 1

2   a   How many thirds are in one whole?

     b   How many quarters are in one whole?

     c   How many sixths are in one whole?

You can say whether a fraction is bigger or smaller than a half.

3 Draw this table in your book so that it fills up a page.

Less than a half	Equal to a half	More than a half

Write the fractions from **question I** in the table.

Challenge
Write as many fractions as you can in the different parts of the diagram.

Fractions, decimals, %, ratio and proportion 4

You can use division to find a fraction of a number.

⚠ Fraction models

You will need interlocking cubes of different colours.

> To find $\frac{1}{3}$ divide by 3.
> To find $\frac{1}{4}$ divide by 4.
> To find $\frac{1}{5}$ divide by 5.

1   Make a cat out of 24 cubes.
    The shape of your cat might look like this:
    Work out from the fractions below how
    many cubes of each colour to use.
    Show your working like this:

$$\frac{1}{4} \text{ of } 24 = 24 \div 4$$
$$24 \div 4 = 6$$
$$6 \text{ blue cubes}$$

a $\frac{1}{4}$ of the cat should be blue.
b $\frac{1}{3}$ of the cat should be green.
c $\frac{1}{6}$ of the cat should be yellow.
d $\frac{1}{4}$ of the cat should be red.

Check that you have used 24 cubes altogether.

2   Now make a cat out of 30 cubes.
    Work out from the fractions how many cubes of each colour to use.
    a $\frac{1}{5}$ of the cat should be white.
    b $\frac{1}{6}$ of the cat should be green.
    c $\frac{1}{3}$ of the cat should be blue.
    d $\frac{1}{10}$ of the cat should be orange.
    e $\frac{1}{5}$ of the cat should be black.

You can use division to find a fraction of a number.

▣ What's the fraction?

You will need interlocking cubes of different colours.

1   Make the shape of a house out of 40 cubes. Work out from the fractions below how many cubes of each colour to use. Show your working like this:

$\frac{1}{4}$ of 40 = 40 ÷ 4
40 ÷ 4 = 10
10 blue cubes

a $\frac{1}{4}$ of the house should be blue.
b $\frac{1}{8}$ of the house should be orange.
c $\frac{1}{8}$ of the house should be yellow.
d $\frac{1}{5}$ of the house should be green.
e $\frac{1}{5}$ of the house should be black.
f $\frac{1}{10}$ of the house should be white.

Check that you have used a total of 40 cubes.

To find what fraction of the hat is black:
count how many cubes altogether: 18.
Now count how many black cubes: 9.
9 is $\frac{1}{2}$ of 18.
The hat is $\frac{1}{2}$ black.

2   a   What fraction of the hat is brown?
    b   What fraction is white?

3   a   What fraction of the boat is brown?
    b   What fraction is yellow?

➤

You can use division to find a fraction of a number.

4 What fraction of the car is:
   a black
   b red
   c yellow
   d blue
   e green?

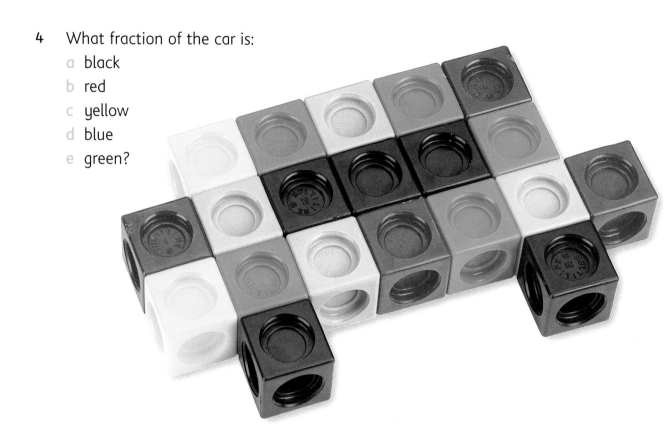

5 Make three of your own models using 30 cubes.
   For each model you make, record the cubes you use in a table like this:

Colour	Number of cubes	Fraction of total
red	5	$30 \div 5 = 6$, so $\frac{1}{6}$ are red

Fractions, decimals, %, ratio and proportion 5

You can use division to solve problems involving fractions.

⚠ Problems with fractions

You will need RS 32.

1 These items have been reduced in a half-price sale. Write the new prices in your book.

2 A sweet shop is offering $\frac{1}{3}$ extra free on the mass of their pick-and-mix sweets.
   a How much heavier will the sweet bags be if they are $\frac{1}{3}$ heavier?

   b What is the mass of the sweets now?

3 A class of 32 children does a survey to find out about favourite foods.

   $\frac{1}{4}$ of the class likes chips best.
   $\frac{1}{8}$ likes fruit best.
   $\frac{1}{2}$ likes chocolate best.

   How many children chose:
   a chips   b chocolate   c fruit   d something else?

   Record your answers on RS 32.

You can use division to solve problems involving fractions.

4   A giant cat is 90 cm tall.
    A pet kitten is $\frac{1}{10}$ of this height.
    How tall is the kitten?

5   These survey results show 40 children's favourite types of TV programmes:
    $\frac{1}{10}$ like nature programmes
    $\frac{1}{5}$ like sports programmes
    $\frac{1}{4}$ like cartoons
    $\frac{1}{5}$ like films
    $\frac{1}{4}$ like comedy programmes

    a How many children like sports programmes best?
    b How many children like nature programmes best?
    c How many children did not choose nature programmes?

6   Ms Pipe the car sales assistant had 120 cars.
    She sold $\frac{1}{3}$ of them last week.

    a How many cars did she sell?
    b How many cars did she have left?
    c $\frac{1}{5}$ of the customers who bought a car last week complained about the cars.
       How many complained?
    d She sells the same fraction of cars every week.
       How long does it take her to sell all the cars?

You can use division to solve problems involving fractions.

回 Take away fractions

You will need RS 32.

1/3 OFF THESE PRICES!

Noodles	£3.60
Sweet and Sour pork	£3.90
Seaweed	£1.20
Rice	£0.90
Spare ribs	£4.20
Prawns	£6.00
Sweetcorn soup	£2.40
Spring rolls	60p each
Special menu for 4	£12.00

This Chinese takeaway restaurant has reduced its prices by $\frac{1}{3}$.

1   Write the total cost of these takeaway orders with the new lower prices.
    Use the steps on RS 32 to help you.

Remember to take away $\frac{1}{3}$ from the price that you see!

2   Which order was the most expensive?

Order A

1 noodles
1 rice
1 spare ribs
2 spring rolls

Order B

3 pork sweet and sour
2 prawns
4 spring rolls
1 special menu

Order C

2 soups
1 special menu
2 seaweed
2 noodles
2 rice

Order D

2 special menus
3 pork sweet and sour
3 spare ribs
6 spring rolls

You can order fractions using symbols.

◎ **Less than or more than?**

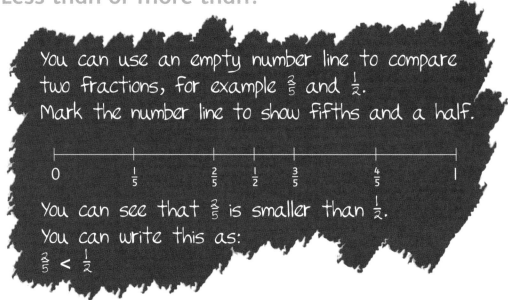

You can use an empty number line to compare two fractions, for example $\frac{2}{5}$ and $\frac{1}{2}$.

Mark the number line to show fifths and a half.

You can see that $\frac{2}{5}$ is smaller than $\frac{1}{2}$.

You can write this as:

$\frac{2}{5} < \frac{1}{2}$

1 Write these pairs of fractions in your book.

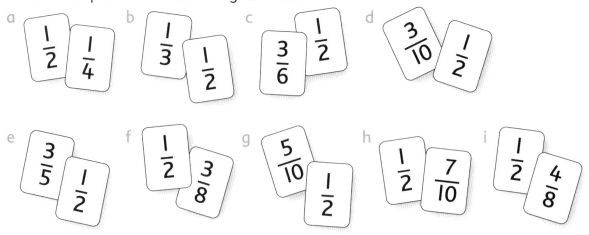

a $\frac{1}{2}$ $\frac{1}{4}$

b $\frac{1}{3}$ $\frac{1}{2}$

c $\frac{3}{6}$ $\frac{1}{2}$

d $\frac{3}{10}$ $\frac{1}{2}$

e $\frac{3}{5}$ $\frac{1}{2}$

f $\frac{1}{2}$ $\frac{3}{8}$

g $\frac{5}{10}$ $\frac{1}{2}$

h $\frac{1}{2}$ $\frac{7}{10}$

i $\frac{1}{2}$ $\frac{4}{8}$

Use an empty number line to find out which is bigger.
If the fractions are equal, put the symbol = between them.
If the fractions are not equal put the symbol < or > between them to show which is bigger.

You can order fractions using symbols.

🔁 Fractions sorted

1   Copy this table in your book.

$< \frac{1}{2}$	$> \frac{1}{2}$	$= \frac{1}{2}$

Put these fractions into the table, deciding whether they are:
less than $\frac{1}{2}$ (<) or more than $\frac{1}{2}$ (>) or equal to $\frac{1}{2}$ (=).

2   Write fractions to make these statements true.

a $\frac{1}{2} >$ ____   b $\frac{1}{2} <$ ____   c ____ $> \frac{1}{2}$

d $\frac{1}{2} =$ ____   e ____ $< \frac{1}{2}$ f ____ $= \frac{1}{2}$

You can write tenths as decimals.

⚠ Fraction changer

This machine changes fractions to decimals.

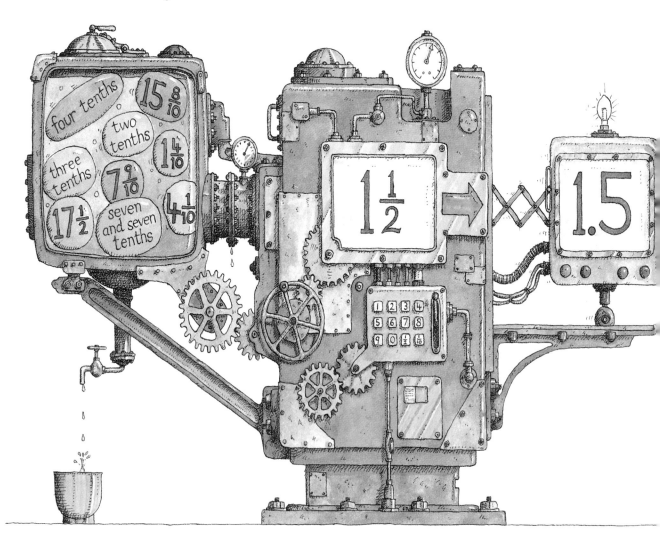

1   Write out the decimal numbers that you make like this: $1\frac{1}{2} = 1.5$

The first one has been done for you.

You can write tenths as decimals.

2   Draw this table in your books.

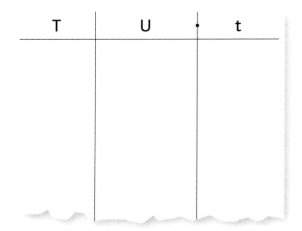

T	U	.	t

a Write the decimals that you made in **question 1**, in the table.
b Write the decimals in a list, starting with the smallest.

3   For each number, what is the value of the digit in red?

You can write tenths as decimals.

◎ Changing fractions and decimals

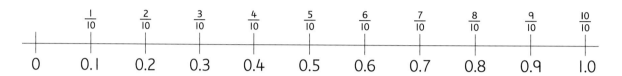

1   Can you match the decimal to its fraction?
    One has been done for you.

2   Change these fractions to decimals.
     a one tenth   b $\frac{5}{10}$ c $2\frac{3}{10}$ d $3\frac{7}{10}$
     e seven tenths   f one and two tenths   g six and four tenths

3   Change these decimal numbers to fraction numbers.
    How many tenths in each?
     a 8.2   b 7.9   c 6.5   d 4.4
     e 9.3   f 2.1   g 18.6   h 25.7

Fractions, decimals, %, ratio and proportion 8

You can write tenths as decimals.

Decimals to fractions

1 Write these decimals as fractions.

	Tens	Units	tenths
a		3	2
b	1	2	9
c	7	5	6
d		0	8
e		9	7
f	1	4	5
g	3	3	3
h	9	0	1

e.g. a) $3\frac{2}{10}$

2 Change these fractions to decimals.

a $32\frac{3}{10}$ b $29\frac{5}{10}$ c $16\frac{4}{10}$

d $75\frac{6}{10}$ e $51\frac{1}{10}$ f $93\frac{7}{10}$

g $13\frac{1}{2}$ h $84\frac{8}{10}$ i $212\frac{2}{10}$

3 Write the decimal numbers from **question 2** in ascending order.
Put them in a place value grid – draw one in your book.

H	T	U	t

Ascending order means sorting from the smallest number to the largest.

You can count in tenths to find the difference between two decimal fractions

回 Decimal spells

1   How can you get from the first number to the second number in one step?
    Show how you worked it out.

$$4.7 + 0.2 = 4.9$$

a 4.7   4.9   b 6.5   6.1   c 7.5   7.75

d 9.5   9.1   e 12.6   13.1   f 14.9   14.2

g 0.9   1.8   h 1.25   1.75   i 2.25   3.0

2   How can you get from the first number to the second number in two steps?
    Show how you worked it out. The first one is done for you.

          −0.5   −0.5

a 8.5   8   7.5   b 8.2 to 7.8
c 4.5 to 5.3   d 5.6 to 6.8
e 9.7 to 0.8   f 12.3 to 9.9
g 16.4 to 14.8   h 14.2 to 12.3

Challenge

In how many different ways can you change:
- 10 to 8.2
- 11.5 to 13.7?

Investigate the largest and smallest number of steps possible.

Fractions, decimals, %, ratio and proportion 10

You can use decimals to change centimetres to metres.

⚠ How far into the pyramid?

Yasmin Rahman is at point A. Guide her to point I by writing how far to travel between each point.

1   Work out in centimetres how far she needs to travel between each point to get from A to E.

a) A to B   5.8 m
b) B to C   3.5 m
c) C to D   4.9 m
d) D to E   2.2 m

2   Work out in metres how far she needs to travel to get from E to I.

a) E to F   990 cm
b) F to G   420 cm
c) G to H   380 cm
d) H to I   750 cm

Challenge

1   What was the shortest distance Yasmin travelled?

2   What was the longest distance Yasmin travelled?

You can use decimals to change centimetres to metres.

◎ Measuring Mummy

Here are some mummies that have been found in a tomb.

1 Change the lengths of the mummies to centimetres.
  Copy and continue the table in your book.

Length of mummy	
Metres	Centimetres
0.3 m	30 cm
0.2 m	

2 Some more mummies were found in the next-door tomb.
  They were measured in centimetres.
  a Add these measurements to the centimetre column in your book.

   170 cm   120 cm   130 cm   40 cm   60 cm

  b Write these measurements as metres.

You can use decimals to change centimetres to metres.

🔲 Pyramid centimetre trail

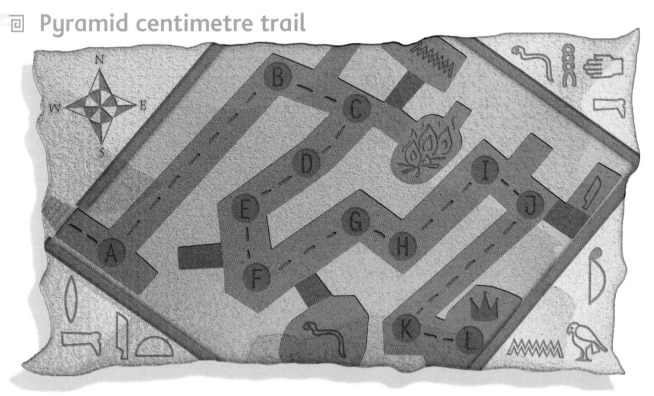

The archaeologist doesn't want to get lost in the pyramid.
As she explores, she leaves a string of centimetre cubes so that she can find her way out.

1   How many centimetre cubes does she leave from:
    a   A to B   8.75 m   b   B to C   6.9 m   c   C to D   7.5 m
    d   D to E   3.25 m   e   E to F   0.8 m   f   F to G   5.7 m.

2   How many metres of centimetre cubes does she need to get from:
    a   G to H   110 cm   b   H to I   340 cm   c   I to J   225 cm
    d   J to K   1210 cm   e   K to L   190 cm.

3   a   How far did she travel in cm from B to D?
    b   How far did she travel in cm from E to G?
    c   How far did she travel in m from G to I?

You can solve problems with money by changing pounds to pence.

⚠ Running totals

You will need:

- a partner
- a piece of paper
- RS 51.

Play the prices game on RS 51.

You each have £10 pocket money to spend in the toy shop.

Challenge

1 Round all items to the nearest pound.

2 Assume that you can only buy one of each item.
   a What is the fewest number of items that you can buy for £10? What are they?
   b What is the greatest number of items that you can buy for £10? What are they?

You can solve problems with money by changing pounds to pence.

◎ Add the prices

You will need:
- a partner
- a piece of paper
- RS 51.

Play the prices game on RS 51.
You each have £5 pocket money to spend in the toy shop.

Challenge

What is the greatest number of items you can buy for £5? List them.

You can solve problems with money by changing pounds to pence.

▣ Spending money

You will need:
- a partner
- a piece of paper
- RS 51.

Play the prices game on RS 51.
You each have £20 to spend in the toy shop.

marbles — 65p each
balloons — 179p
book — £3.50
alien — £1.40
rubber snakes — £1.20
wand — 35p
pack of cards — £1.90
pencils — 60p
stickers — £0.80
travel game — £4.50
bracelet — £2.21
maths sets — 250p

Challenge

1   Round all items to the nearest pound.

2   Assume that you can only buy one of each item.
   a Can you work out how many different ways you can spend exactly £20?
   b What is the fewest number of items that you can buy for £20? What are they?
   c What is the greatest number of items that you can buy for £20? What are they?

You can solve problems using proportion.

⚠ Buy one, get one free

1   For every two cookies you buy, you get one free!
   a   How many cookies do you get free if you buy four cookies?
   b   How many cookies do you get free if you buy six cookies?
   c   How many cookies do you get free if you buy eight cookies?
   d   You want 15 cookies altogether. How many do you need to pay for?

2   For every bottle of shampoo you buy, you get one free!
   a   How many bottles will you pay for if you want four bottles?
   b   How many bottles will you pay for if you want eight bottles?
   c   You have six bottles in your shopping basket.
      How many bottles do you get free?

3   Buy five yoghurts, get two free.
   How many yoghurts do you get free if you buy:
   a   10 yoghurts
   b   15 yoghurts
   c   20 yoghurts?

4   For every three notebooks you buy, you get one free pencil.
   a   How many notebooks do you need to buy if you
      want two pencils?
   b   How many notebooks do you need to buy if you
      want three pencils?
   c   I buy 12 notebooks. How many pencils do I get free?

5   In every week, the supermarket is open for six days.
   How many days is it open in:
   a   two weeks
   b   four weeks
   c   ten weeks?

You can solve problems using proportion.

▣ Special offers

1 For every two cakes you buy, you get one cake free.
   a How many cakes do you need to buy to get five free?
   b Julie puts 12 cakes in her shopping basket.
   How many will she get free?

2 Buy three bags of poppadoms and get one jar of chutney free.
   a How many bags would you buy to get three free
   jars of chutney?
   b I buy seven bags of poppadoms and get two free jars.
   How many more bags would I need to get another
   free jar?
   c A manager of a restaurant makes a big purchase.
   He gets 14 free jars of chutney.
   How many bags of poppadoms did he buy?

3 In every bag of seven apples, two are free.
   a How many apples in eight bags?
   b How many apples do you get free if you buy seven bags?

4 For every seven stickers in a pack you get two shiny stickers.
   a Sam has 14 shiny stickers. How many packs did he buy?
   b How many stickers does Sam have altogether?
   c Meera has a collection of 189 stickers.
   How many shiny stickers has she got?

5 Mrs Ling needs to buy 30 gifts for the children in her class.
   She cannot decide what to buy. Which gift should
   Mrs Ling buy so that she spends
   the least amount of money?
   Show how you worked it out.

Pencil
Sharpeners
36p

Pencils 45p
buy 2 get 1 free

Glitter pens 7
buy 1 get 1 free

You can use different words to say 'add' or 'subtract'.

⚠ Make up a number sentence

Use these numbers to answer the questions below.

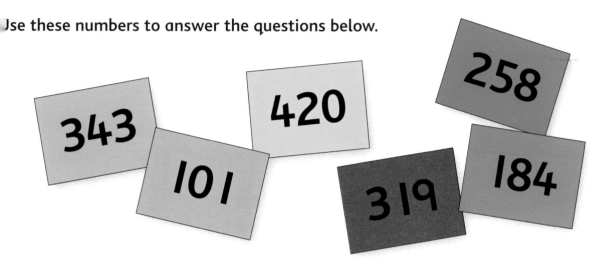

1   Write one addition and one subtraction sentence for each number above.
    For example:

$$236 + 107 = 343$$
$$400 - 57 = 343$$

2   Look at RS 66. Use this to help you rewrite each number sentence from above using a
    suitable word or phrase instead of the symbols. Underline the words that mean add
    or subtract and write what they mean.

    236 <u>plus</u> 107 is 343   plus means add
    <u>Decrease</u> 400 by 57   decrease means take away

    Try to use a different phrase for each sentence.

You can use different words to say 'add' or 'subtract'.

◎ **Make up a question**

Use these numbers to answer the questions below.

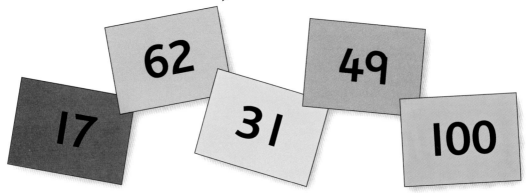

I   Write one addition and one subtraction sentence for each number above.
    For example:

    14 + 3 = 17
    20 − 3 = 17

2   Look at RS 66. Use this to help you rewrite each number sentence from above using a
    suitable word or phrase instead of the symbols. Underline the words that mean
    add or subtract.
    For example:

    Increase 14 by 3   increase means add
    Decrease 20 by 3   decrease means take away

    Try to use a different phrase for each sentence.

You can use different words to say 'add' or 'subtract'.

Addition and subtraction sentences

Use these numbers to answer the questions below.

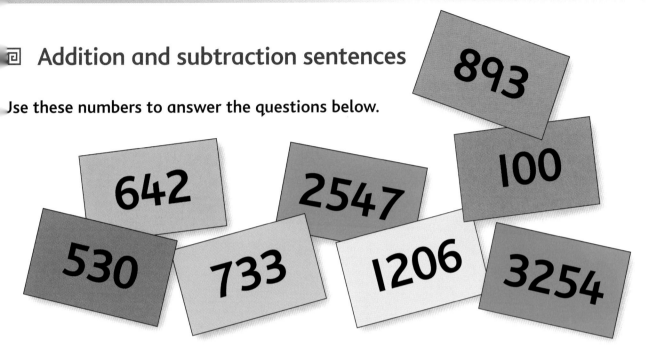

1   Write one addition and one subtraction sentence for each number above.
    For example:

$$250 + 280 = 530$$
$$600 - 70 = 530$$

2   Look at RS 66. Use this to help you rewrite each number sentence from above using a
    suitable word or phrase instead of the symbols. Underline the words that mean add
    or subtract and write what they mean.
    For example:

The <u>sum of</u> 250 and 280   the sum of means add
<u>How many fewer</u> is 70 than 600?   how many fewer means
                                        take away

Try to use a different phrase for each sentence.

You can use jottings to help calculate when adding or subtracting.

⚠ How will you work it out?

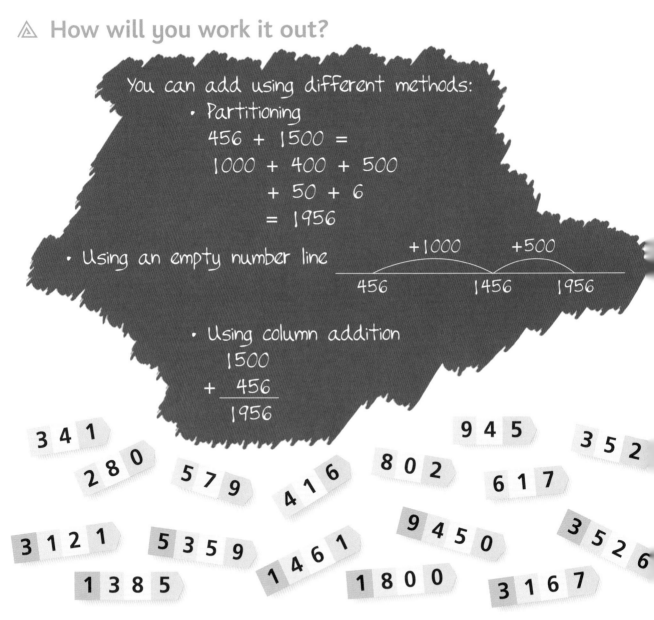

You can add using different methods:
- Partitioning
  456 + 1500 =
  1000 + 400 + 500
  + 50 + 6
  = 1956

- Using an empty number line

  +1000   +500
  456   1456   1956

- Using column addition
  1500
  + 456
  1956

341 280 579 416 802 945 352 617
3121 5359 1461 9450 3526
1385 1800 3167

1 a Choose a 3-digit number and a 4-digit number from the place value cards.
   b Decide how you will add the numbers.
     Find their total. Show your working out in your book.
   c Repeat until you have added five pairs of numbers.

2 Repeat **question 1**, but this time subtract the 3-digit number from the 4-digit number.

You can use jottings to help calculate when adding or subtracting.

Digit banks

You will need RS 68.

Use numbers from the number banks.

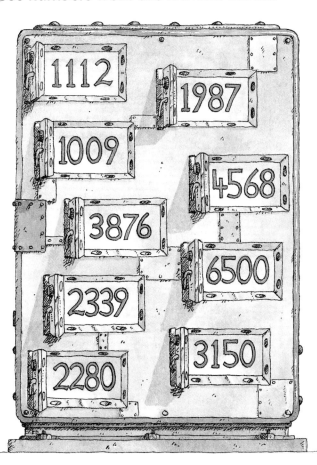

1   On RS 68, place a 4-digit number in each oval shape.

2   Place a 3-digit number in each square shape.

3   Solve your problems.

4   Show how you worked out the answers.

You can carry out mental calculations of addition and subtraction facts quickly.

 Quick fire

You will need:
- a group of three players
- a set of number cards.

Quick fire addition

Game rules

- For each round, one person is the dealer and the other two are the players.
- The dealer shuffles the cards thoroughly.
- They deal two cards face up onto the table so that the players can see both of them.
- The first player to say the **total** of the cards correctly wins them.
- If both players say the correct answer together, they get one card each.
- Both players check the calculation on a number line.
- The round ends either after 2 minutes or when all the cards have been used.
- The winner is the player with more cards.

Quickly gather up the cards. Play the next round with a new dealer.

Quick fire subtraction

Game rules

The rules are the same as for **Quick fire addition**, but this time the players **find the difference** between the numbers on the cards.

You can quickly double numbers using a range of strategies.

⚠ How will you double?

You can use partitioning to help double:

2300

2000 + 2000   300 + 300

4000   +   600   = 4600

This number doubler can usually double numbers up to 10 000. It is not working today.

1   Double these numbers for the machine. Work out the quickest way to double each number. Show how you worked it out.

    a 450   b 49   c 600   d 330   e 37   f 160
    g 250   h 1100   i 2400   j 28   k 590   l 2350

2   Explain two strategies that you used to double.

3   Try to double some of your answers from **question 1**.
    Which are difficult to double? Why?

You can quickly double numbers using a range of strategies.

▣ Correct the doubles

1 Daniel and Sohil have been doubling numbers.
Check their work to see if they have been
doubling correctly.
Write the calculations out in your book.
If their answer is wrong, give the correct answer.

> You can use doubles
> you already know to
> help you double other
> numbers. For example:
>
> double 16 = 32
> double 160 = 320
> double 1600 = 3200

  a   360 + 360 = 702 ✗ 360 + 360 = 600 + 120 = 720

  b   38 + 38 = 66

  c   4900 + 4900 = 81 800

  d   230 + 230 = 460

  e   590 + 590 = 1080

  f   3400 + 3400 = 6880

  g   2700 + 2700 = 5280

  h   28 + 28 = 56

  i   1800 + 1800 = 2600

  j   710 + 710 = 1240

2 Write two more doubles for each double fact.
    a double 12 = 24   b double 36 = 72   c double 19 = 38
    d double 49 = ?   e double 38 = ?   f double 27 = ?

You can find number pairs up to 100 or 1000 quickly.

⚠ Number pairs

Here is a set of test results. There were 100 questions in the test.

1 Work out how many answers were wrong each time.

Test results

a 97 out of 100. **3** answers were wrong

b 45 out of 100.

c 67 out of 100.

d 33 out of 100.

e 24 out of 100.

f 12 out of 100.

g 94 out of 100.

h 86 out of 100.

i 59 out of 100.

j 71 out of 100.

k 88 out of 100.

l 35 out of 100.

> Use what you know about pairs of numbers that total 100.

This table shows how many points were given to every class in a school.

Class	Red	Green	Yellow	Blue	Orange	Brown	Violet
Points	250	650	450	350	150	550	50

2 They need to get 1000 points to receive a class prize.

a Work out how many points each class needs to get to reach 1000 points.

b Check your answers by adding together the pairs of numbers that you found.

Mental calculation strategies (+ and −) 1

You can add and subtract multiples of 10 and 100 by counting on or back in tens and hundreds.

⚠ **How many miles?**

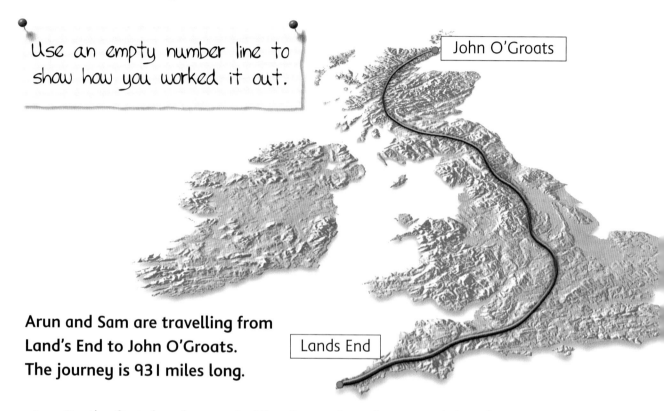

Use an empty number line to show how you worked it out.

John O'Groats

Lands End

Arun and Sam are travelling from Land's End to John O'Groats. The journey is 931 miles long.

1   On the first day they cycle 43 miles and on the second day they walk 20 miles. How far have they travelled by the end of the second day?

2   After six days they have travelled 633 miles. On Day 7 they fly 200 miles by helicopter. How far have they travelled altogether at the end of Day 7?

3   On Day 8 they travel 60 miles by boat. How far have they travelled altogether by the end of Day 8?

4   The next morning they travel by scooter. They stop for lunch. A friend tells them that they have a further 20 miles to travel to get to John O'Groats.
    a   How far did they travel in the morning?
    b   How far have they travelled so far?

Mental calculation strategies (+ and −) 4

You can add several numbers quickly by looking for pairs that add up to make easier numbers.

⚠ Grids of numbers

1   Find the line of four numbers, horizontal, vertical or diagonal, with the highest total.

2   Find the square of four numbers with the lowest total.

13	6	3	14
2	12	3	5
7	9	11	4
15	8	1	16

3   Find the totals of the rows and columns.

4   Find the totals of three different squares of four numbers.

10	60	20
50	90	70
40	80	30

5   Find the totals of the rows and columns.

6   Find the totals of three different squares of four numbers.
    Show how you found these totals.

600	900	500
800	200	300
100	700	400

➤ Mental calculation strategies (+ and −) 4

You can add several numbers quickly by looking for pairs that add up to make easier numbers.

◎ Add three cards

You will need:
- a partner
- a set of cards numbered 1 – 15
- a set of cards numbered 1 – 10.

1   Shuffle the cards and place both sets in a stack facing downwards.

2   Take turns to pick three cards from the stack.

3   Find the total of the numbers on the cards. Look for two cards that make an 'easy' total to add first.

4   Write down the total of your set of three cards in a table like the one below.

Jane	Points	Sammi	Points
4 + 6 + 5 = 15	10	7 + 3 + 14 = 24	10
8 + 8 + 6 = 22	2	9 + 10 + 7 = 26	5

5   Continue playing until you run out of cards.

6   When you have finished the round, work out your scores as shown above.
- Score 10 points for each sum where the first two numbers you added made a multiple of 10.
- Score 5 points for each sum where the first two numbers you added made a near multiple of 10.
- Score 2 points for each sum where the first two numbers you added were a double.

7   Play the game again until one player reaches 100. This player is the winner.

► Mental calculation strategies (+ and −) 4

You can add several numbers quickly by looking for pairs that add up to make easier numbers.

🔁 Patterns in addition

1   Find the total of all the numbers from 0 to 10. See if you can find a quick way of doing it.

2   What is the total of the even numbers from 0 to 10?

3   Look for quick ways of finding these totals:
   a   0 to 20
   b   0 to 50
   c   multiples of 10 from 0 to 100
   d   multiples of 100 from 0 to 1000
   e   multiples of 3 from 0 to 30

4   What strategies did you use for finding these totals?

Mental calculation strategies (+ and −) 5

You can find a small difference by counting up on a number line.

⚠ Numbers with small differences

Work with a partner.

1   Use each digit card above once to make two 3-digit numbers with a small difference.

2   Calculate the difference.

3   What is the smallest difference that you can make using these cards?

4   Make the pair of three-digit numbers with the smallest difference using the set of cards above. Show all of your calculations.

5   Use the digit cards above to make the pair of four-digit numbers with the smallest difference.

6   What strategies do you use to find numbers that are close to each other?

► Mental calculation strategies (+ and −) 5

You can find a small difference by counting up on a number line.

🔲 Difference of seven

You will need a set of 0-9 digit cards.

1   Make pairs of 3-digit numbers that have a difference of 7.
    You may only use each card once in each pair of numbers.
    e.g.

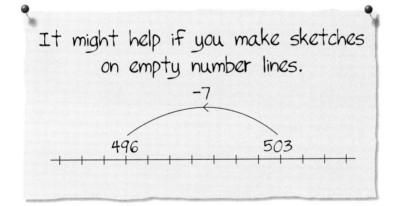

It might help if you make sketches
on empty number lines.

2   How many different pairs can you make?

3   How many different pairs can you make that have a difference of less than 7?

4   Can you make a pair of 4-digit numbers with a difference of 7?

5   What cards would you need to add to the set?
    Using the cards that you added, how many can you make now?

You can work out differences by counting up on a number line.

⚠ Making complements

You will need:
- a calculator
- any 30 cards from a shuffled 0 – 100 pack
- a set of cards made from RS 89.

We need to add **66**

Work with a partner.

1 　🖩 Take a card from the 0–100 pack.
　　Enter the number into the calculator.

2 　Agree with your partner the number that you
　　should add on the calculator to make a total of 100.

3 　Add the number and check that you were correct.

4 　Leave this number in the calculator.

5 　Take another card from the pack and add it to the total
　　on the calculator. Then decide what to add to make 200.

6 　Add that number.

7 　Keep adding a number from the pack and the
　　number needed to make the next multiple of 100.

8 　When you reach 1000, continue the activity using the cards made from RS 89.

9 　Keep a record of your work. You might record it like this.

Mental calculation strategies (+ and −) 6

You can work out differences by counting up on a number line.

◎ Word problems

1   Mrs Thompson's class is growing sunflowers.
    The children are having a competition to see
    whose sunflower grows to 100 cm first.
    How much taller do they each have to grow
    to reach 100 cm?

    34 cm Liz   46 cm Rashid   52 cm Andrew

2   In the music shop the CDs come in boxes of 100.
    Tom is checking how many CDs are left and how many have been sold.
    Copy and complete the table that Tom started.

CD title	Number in the box	Number sold
Classical sounds	47	
Rock 'n' roll hits	28	
Pop classics		51
Scottish country music	65	

3   Bhavik has £100 for his birthday. These are the things that he likes in the shop.

digital camera £39

radio £13

portable TV £86

How much will Bhavik have left if he buys:

a   the radio
b   the CD
c   the television
d   the remote controlled car?

remote controlled car £73

➤ Mental calculation strategies (+ and −) 6

You can work out differences by counting up on a number line.

▣ Dice games

You will need:
- a partner
- three 0 – 6 dice
- scrap paper.

1 Write the multiples of 100 up to 900 on a piece of scrap paper.

2 Shake the three dice and use the dice scores as the digits in a 3-digit number.

3 Choose a multiple of 100 from the scrap paper and find the difference between your two numbers using a number line.

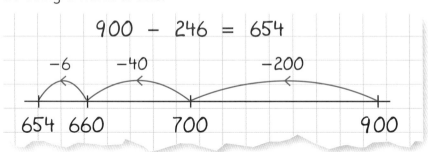

$$900 - 246 = 654$$

4 Record your calculation and cross the multiple of 100 off the list.

5 Take turns to find differences in the same way until you have each had four goes.

6 Write the differences that you both calculated in ascending order.

Challenge
Repeat the game using four dice to make 4-digit numbers and using a list of multiples of 1000.

You can use doubles to add two numbers that are close to each other.

△ ▣ Near doubles

You will need:

- a partner
- a watch.

1. How quickly can you work out the answers to these 'near doubles' questions?
Work in pairs and get your partner to time you.

a 37 + 35   b 15 + 14

c 28 + 26   d 130 + 150

e 245 + 247   f 233 + 231

g 18 + 19   h 44 + 51

i 490 + 500   j 225 + 226

2. Tommy and Alisha have answered some 'near doubles' questions and explained their methods. Find the answer on a flash card that goes with each method below.

3.
a Double 40 then subtract 4   b Double 25

c Double 300 then add 20   d Double 500 then subtract 5

e Double 250 then subtract 20   f Double 20 then subtract 2

g Double 160 then add 10   h Double 360

☐ + ☐ = 76

☐ + ☐ = 720

☐ + ☐ = 50

☐ + ☐ = 330

☐ + ☐ = 480

☐ + ☐ = 995

☐ + ☐ = 620

☐ + ☐ = 38

4. Make up a 'near doubles' question that could go with each calculation on the flash cards, e.g. 36 + 40 = 76.

You can use doubles to add two numbers that are close to each other.

◎ I know that ...

Use information you already know to help you work out three or more addition facts.

Write your facts in your book. The first one is done for you.

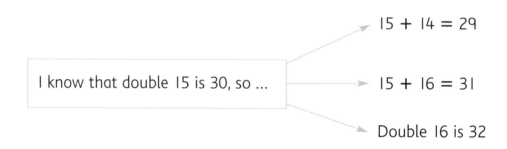

I know that double 15 is 30, so ...

15 + 14 = 29

15 + 16 = 31

Double 16 is 32

1   I know that double 100 is 200, so ...

2   I know that double 30 is 60, so ...

3   I know that double 150 is 300, so ...

4   I know that double 12 is 24, so ...

5   I know that double 20 is 40, so ...

6   I know that double 210 is 420, so ...

7   I know that double 140 is 280, so ...

8   I know that double 40 is 80, so ...

You can use near doubles to add consecutive numbers.

⚠ Consecutive numbers and near doubles

> Consecutive numbers are numbers that are
> next door to each other in a sequence,
> for example, 0 and 2, 2 and 4
> are consecutive even numbers

1   Add all the pairs of consecutive numbers from the racing cars.

2   What do you notice about your answers?

3   Say whether you think these statements are true or false. Explain your reasons.
   a When you add two consecutive even numbers the answer is always an even number.
   b You can make any even number by adding two consecutive even numbers.
   c The sum of two consecutive even numbers is a multiple of 4.

4   Add all the numbers from the racing cars below.

5   What statements can you make about the sums of consecutive odd numbers?

You can use near doubles to add consecutive numbers.

◎ Adding consecutive numbers

8 and 9 are consecutive numbers. Their sum is 17.

Use the numbers from 1 to 20.

1 Find other pairs of consecutive numbers.

2 Work out the sum of each pair.

3 What do you notice about your answers?

Near doubles will help you find all the consecutive number sums.

You can choose calculation strategies that suit the numbers in the calculation.

▣ Choosing strategies

You will need:

- a copy of RS 94 cut into 12 cards
- a large copy of the strategy chart RS 93.

Work with a partner.

1   Choose any two cards from RS 94 and find their sum and difference.

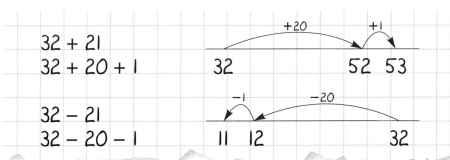

2   Record your calculation under one of the strategy headings in the chart on RS 93.

3   Repeat for other pairs of cards.

4   Which strategies do you use most?

5   Which do you use least?

6   Which numbers do the different strategies work best for?

7   Write a sentence in each box on the chart that starts like this.

I use this strategy when...

Pencil and paper procedures (+ and −) 2

You can find the best way to add numbers by looking at the calculation first

⚠ Finding additions

You will need 1-9 digit cards.

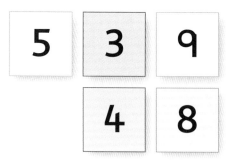

1   Shuffle your cards and
    deal out five like this.

2   Record the numbers and use columns to add them.

3   Mix up these five numbers and repeat until you have made six different addition
    calculations. Solve all the additions.

4   a Are any of your answers in **question 3** the same?
    b If there is a matching pair, can you explain why they match?
    c If no pair of answers is the same, try to make a pair that matches.

5   a Shuffle and deal out another set of five cards.
    b Find as many additions as you can, that have the same answer.
       How many additions did you find?

◎ Adding in columns

```
  62          6 2
+ 26
              2 6
```

> Look at the numbers in the
> calculation before you choose
> which way to add.

Use columns to add the pairs of numbers.

62 26	47 36	74 53	103 35	257 41

155   43

Pencil and paper procedures (+ and −) 6

You can find a difference between two numbers, by counting up from the lower to the higher number and recording the 'jumps' in columns to add them easily.

◰ Finding the difference

You will need some 0-9 digit cards.

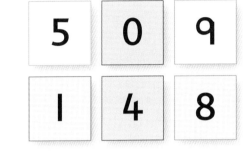

1 Shuffle your cards and deal out six.
   Make two 3-digit numbers.
   a Try to count up in your head from the
      lower number to the higher number
      and write down the difference.
   b Record the calculation and use columns to find the difference.
   c Repeat a and b for three more pairs of numbers.

2 Dwayne found a quicker way to find a difference.
   What calculation did he start with?

$$+ \quad 24 \rightarrow 200$$
$$+ 200 \rightarrow 400$$
$$+ \quad 45 \rightarrow 445$$
$$\overline{\quad 269 \quad}$$

3 a Follow these steps to investigate the difference
      between at least five pairs of numbers.
      • Make a 3-digit number.
      • Reverse it.
      • Use columns to find the difference between
        the two numbers.

$$\begin{array}{r} 9\ 4\ 2 \\ -\ 2\ 4\ 9 \\ \hline \end{array}$$
$$+ \quad 5\ 1 \rightarrow 300$$
$$+ 6\ 0\ 0 \rightarrow 900$$
$$+ \quad 4\ 2 \rightarrow 942$$
$$\overline{\quad 6\ 9\ 3 \quad}$$

   Remember to put the larger number first.

   b Look at your answers to 3a. Write what you notice about:
      • the middle number
      • the first and last digits?
   c Can you use your answer to 3b to predict the answer to 745 − 547?
      Try out some more subtractions like this with a partner.

Pencil and paper procedures (+ and −) 8

You can look at the numbers in a subtraction before you choose which method to use.

⚠ ▣ Vertical subtraction methods

You will need:
- a partner
- RS 113 and cards from RS 115.

- Shuffle the cards and put them face down in a pile.
- Take it in turns to pick a card. Write your name on the card.
- Look at the methods board. Place your card on the method you would use to solve the calculation. (Only one calculation can go on one method.)
- When all the cards are placed, take a card from the board and find the answer using the method on the board.
- Check each other's answers. Score one point for each correct answer.

◎ Vertical methods

You will need:
- a partner
- RS 113 and cards from RS 114.

- Shuffle the cards and put them face down in a pile.
- Take it in turns to pick a card. Write your name on the card.
- Look at the methods board. Place your card on the method you would use to solve the calculation. (Only one calculation can go on one method.)
- When all the cards are placed, take a card from the board and find the answer using the method on the board.
- Check each other's answers. Score one point for each correct answer.

You can adjust the tens when you partition numbers to subtract.

⚠ 回 Changing tens

1   Partition the numbers and subtract the smaller from the larger.

$$
\begin{array}{r}
365 \; - \; 128 \; = \quad 300 \; + \; 50 \; + \; 15 \\
- \quad 100 \; + \; 20 \; + \; 8 \\
\hline
200 \; + \; 30 \; + \; 7 \; = \; 237
\end{array}
$$

a 582   84
b 68   341
c 453   237

d 326   974
e 112   444
f 375   266

2   a Choose three subtractions from **question 1** and record them in columns.

$$
365 \; - \; 128 \; = \quad
\begin{array}{r}
3\;6\;5 \\
-\;1\;2\;8 \\
\hline
\end{array}
\quad = \quad
\begin{array}{r}
3\;5\;{}^{1}5 \\
-\;1\;2\;8 \\
\hline
2\;3\;7
\end{array}
$$

b Check that your answers match your answers from **question 1**.

3

248   576   192   375   467

a Use the numbers on the cards to make four subtractions where you need to adjust from tens to units.
b Find the answers using columns.

You can find remainders when there is not a whole number answer after divisio

◎ **Number line remainders**

You can use a number line to find a remainder after dividing.
21 ÷ 5 =

Jump back from 21 in steps of 5

You can write this as a number sentence: 21 ÷ 5 = 4 R 1

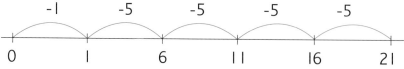

1   Use a number line to jump back in steps of 3.
    Write a number sentence for each division question.
    a 13 ÷ 3   b 16 ÷ 3   c 19 ÷ 3
    d 23 ÷ 3   e 25 ÷ 3

2   Use a number line to jump back in steps of 5.
    a 17 ÷ 5   b 26 ÷ 5   c 31 ÷ 5

Understanding multiplication and division 4

You can round answers up or down after division.

⚠ Dividing pounds

> Think about how you can divide these pounds by splitting the amount in different ways. You could work out £18 ÷ 5 by splitting £18 into £10, £5 and £3.
>
> £10 ÷ 5 = £2   £5 ÷ 5 = £1.00   £3 ÷ 5 = 60p
> £2 + £1.00 + 60p = £3.60

1   £17 ÷ 2

2   £19 ÷ 4

3   £22 ÷ 4

4   £16 ÷ 5

5   £18 ÷ 4

6   £25 ÷ 4

Challenge

An amount of money less than £50 is shared out equally.

If there are two children, £1 is left over.

If there are three children, all the money is shared out.

If there are four children, £1 is left over.

How much money could there be?

➤ Understanding multiplication and division 4

You can round answers up or down after division.

◎ Share the money

1 £7 ÷ 2

2 £9 ÷ 2

3 £10 ÷ 4

4 £11 ÷ 5

5 £13 ÷ 2

Challenge

An amount of money between £20 and £30 is shared out equally.

If there are two children, £1 is left over.

If there are three children, nothing is left over.

If there are four children, £1 is left over.

How much money could there be?

▣ Sharing pounds

1 a £19 ÷ 2   b £27 ÷ 4
   c £26 ÷ 5   d £35 ÷ 4
   e £18 ÷ 10   f £37 ÷ 5

2 Jo gives this amount of money to her friends.
   How much does each friend get when there are:
   a two people
   b four people
   c six people?

Understanding multiplication and division 6

⚠ What's the problem?

Write a number story for each division statement.

You need to think whether your answer:

- is rounded up
- is rounded down
- divides exactly.

These pictures might help you think of some problems.

e.g. $45 \div 6 = 7 \text{ R } 3$
I had 45 sweets. I shared them with 6 friends. We got 7 sweets each with 3 left over. I rounded down.

1 $34 \div 6 = 5 \text{ R } 4$	2 $50 \div 4 = 12 \text{ R } 2$
3 $65 \div 7 = 9 \text{ R } 2$	4 $48 \div 8 = 6$
5 $66 \div 6 = 11$	6 $39 \div 5 = 7 \text{ R } 4$
7 $52 \div 10 = 5 \text{ R } 2$	8 $59 \div 8 = 7 \text{ R } 3$

Challenge

Think of three of your own division statements. Write a number story for each one.

You can round answers up or down after division when solving problems.

◎ Think of a problem

Write a number story for each division statement.

You need to think whether your answer:
- is rounded up
- is rounded down
- divides exactly.

These pictures might help you think of some problems.

e.g. $19 \div 3 = 6 \, R \, 1$
I had 19 stickers. I shared them with 3 friends. We got 6 stickers each with 1 left over. I rounded down.

1 $24 \div 6 = 4$	2 $31 \div 3 = 10 \, R \, 1$
3 $27 \div 4 = 6 \, R \, 3$	4 $32 \div 4 = 8$
5 $38 \div 5 = 7 \, R \, 3$	6 $38 \div 4 = 9 \, R \, 2$
7 $41 \div 10 = 4 \, R \, 1$	8 $36 \div 6 = 6$

Challenge
Think of three of your own division statements. Write a number story for each one.

You can round answers up or down after division when solving problems.

ⓐ Dividing problems

Write a number story for each division statement.

Think about whether the answer:
- is rounded up
- is rounded down
- divides exactly.

These pictures might help you think of some problems.

$90 \div 8 = 11 \, R \, 2$

90 children go on a trip. A minibus holds 8 people. They need 12 buses. I rounded up.

1	$110 \div 10 = 11$	2	$540 \div 6 = 90$	3	$220 \div 10 = 22$
4	$69 \div 7 = 9 \, R \, 6$	5	$84 \div 9 = 9 \, R \, 3$	6	$166 \div 8 = 20 \, R \, 6$
7	$139 \div 7 = 19 \, R \, 6$	8	$364 \div 6 = 60 \, R \, 4$	9	$650 \div 8 = 81 \, R \, 2$

Challenge

Think of three of your own division statements. Write a number story for each one.

Understanding multiplication and division 7

You can explain how addition and multiplication are linked.

⚠ Rectangular arrays

Use cubes to arrange these rectangles. Write down addition number sentences for each rectangle.

1   6 × 3

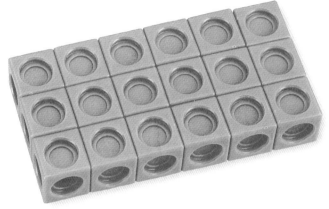

6 + 6 + 6 or
3 + 3 + 3 + 3 + 3 + 3

2   6 × 7

3   9 × 6

4   8 × 7

5   5 × 9

6   7 × 9

Challenge
How many different arrays can you make with 24 cubes? Write all of the number sentences that you can for each array.

You can explain how addition and multiplication are linked.

© Arranging arrays

To work out the number of sweets you can:
• add the number of sweets in each row
  4 + 4 + 4 + 4 + 4 + 4
• add the number of sweets in each column
  6 + 6 + 6 + 6
• multiply the number of sweets in one row by the number of sweets in one column
  4 × 6

6 sweets in a column
4 sweets in a row

Use cubes to arrange these rectangles.
Write down addition number sentences for each rectangle.
The first one is done for you.

| 1 | 4 × 3 |  | 4 + 4 + 4 | 3 + 3 + 3 + 3 |

2 6 × 3   3 4 × 6   4 5 × 4

5 3 × 8   6 5 × 6

Challenge

How many different arrays can you make with 18 cubes?
Write as many number sentences as you can for each array.

You can explain how addition and multiplication are linked.

▣ Calculations and arrays

Write two addition statements and two multiplication statements that describe each array.

1

2

3

4
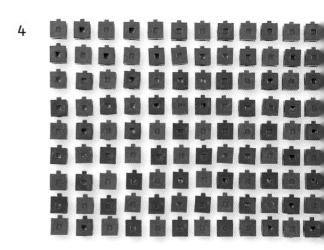

5
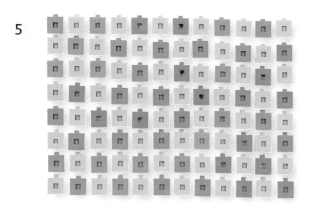

Challenge

Explore how many different arrays could be made with 60 cubes.

Write as many number sentences as you can for each array.

You can use multiplication in a variety of ways to help you work out answers.

⚠ Choose and multiply

1 Choose one number from set A and one number from set B.
   Multiply the two numbers together by writing the calculation in a different way.

Example: 4 and 15
         4 × 15 = 60 could be written as:
         4 × 5 × 3 = 60
         or (10 + 5) × 4 = (10 × 4) + (5 × 4) = 40 + 20

Set A	Set B
3	15
4	25
5	40
6	50

2 Can you explain why the multiplication number sentences give the same answers?

◎ Different ways to multiply

Choose one number from set A and one number from set B from the next page.
Multiply the two numbers together by writing the calculation in a different way.

Example: 3 and 20
         3 × 20 = 60 could be written as:
         3 × 10 × 2 = 60
         or (10 + 10) × 3 = (10 × 3) + (10 × 3) = 60

➤

You can use multiplication in a variety of ways to help you work out answer

Set A
2
3
4
5

Set B
15
20
25
30

▣ Multiply multiples

1 Choose one number from set A and one number from set B.
   Multiply the two numbers by writing the calculation in a different way.

Example: 4 and 40
$4 \times 40 = 160$ could be written as:
$4 \times 2 \times 20 = 160$
or $4 \times (20 + 20) = (4 \times 20) + (4 \times 20) = 80 + 80 = 160$

Set A
6
7
8
9

Set B
25
30
40
45

2 Look back at your answers. Investigate how many different ways you can write each
   multiplication sentence. Use brackets when writing your calculations.

8×40 can be written as:
$8 \times (5 \times 8)$ or $8 \times (10 \times 4)$

Mental calculation strategies (× and ÷) 2

You can multiply by 4 by doubling and doubling again. You can find quarters and eighths by halving.

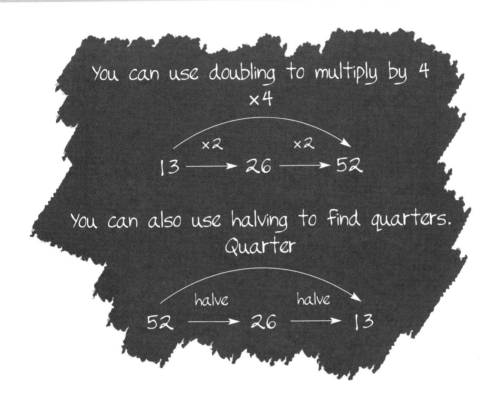

You can use doubling to multiply by 4
×4

13 —×2→ 26 —×2→ 52

You can also use halving to find quarters.
Quarter

52 —halve→ 26 —halve→ 13

⚠ Doubling and halving

Find the missing numbers. Show how you worked them out.

1   36 × 4 = ☐

2   ☐ × 4 = 300

3   $\frac{1}{4}$ of 600 = ☐

4   8 × 29 = ☐

5   $\frac{1}{8}$ of 64 = ☐

6   ☐ × 8 = 300

➤ Mental calculation strategies (× and ÷) 2

You can multiply by 4 by doubling and doubling again. You can find quarters and eighths by halving.

◎ Keep on doubling

Find the missing numbers. Show how you worked them out.

1   $25 \times 4 = \square$

2   $16 \times 4 = \square$

3   $4 \times 18 = \square$

4   $\square \times 4 = 72$

5   $\frac{1}{4}$ of $80 = \square$

◙ Halving again and again ... and again!

Find the missing numbers. Show how you worked them out.

1   $\square \times 4 = 360$

2   $\frac{1}{4}$ of $640 = \square$

3   $36 \times 8 = \square$

4   $\frac{1}{8}$ of $72 = \square$

5   $\frac{1}{8}$ of $112 = \square$

6   $\square \times 8 = 360$

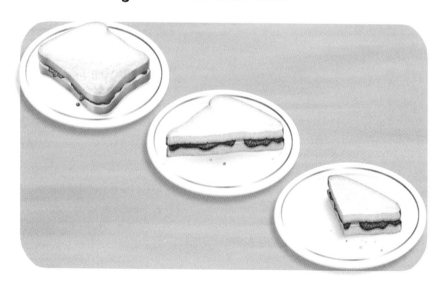

Mental calculation strategies (× and ÷) 4

You can multiply a number by 10 or 100, by moving the digits one or two places to the left.

⚠ Multiplication grids

Copy and complete these multiplication squares.

a

×	72	36
10		
100		

b

×	10	100
51		
		1400

c

×	10	
	160	1600
	100	

▣ More multiplication grids

Copy and complete these multiplication squares.

a

×	10	100
127		
		3600

b

×		
	4700	1000
10	470	

c

×	20	50
300		
		8000

You can multiply a number by 10 or 100, by moving the digits one or two places to the left.

◎ Ten times bigger

When you multiply a number by 10, the digits move one place to the left.

$$36 \times 10 = 360$$

H	T	U	
	3	6	
3	6	0	×10

When you multiply a number by 100, the digits move two places to the left.

$$23 \times 100 = 2300$$

Th	H	T	U	
		2	3	
2	3	0	0	×100

You will need a place value chart.

Answer these questions using a place value chart to help you.

1 $5 \times 10 = \square$

2 $10 \times 3 = \square$

3 $\square \times 10 = 70$

4 $10 \times \square = 60$

5 $100 \times 4 = \square$

6 $7 \times 100 = \square$

7 $100 \times \square = 300$

8 $\square \times 100 = 100$

9 $4 \times \square = 40$

10 $\square \times 9 = 900$

Mental calculation strategies (× and ÷) 7

You can divide a number by 10 or 100, by moving the digits one or two places to the right.

△ ◎ 10 and 100 bingo

You will need:

- a bingo card
- counters.

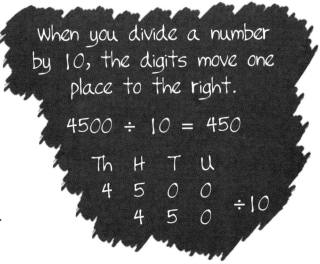

When you divide a number by 10, the digits move one place to the right.

$4500 ÷ 10 = 450$

Th	H	T	U
4	5	0	0
	4	5	0	÷10

1   Take turns to choose a 3-digit multiple of 100 or a 4-digit multiple of 1000. Divide your number by either 10 or 100.

For example: $500 ÷ 100 = 5$
$4000 ÷ 10 = 400$

2   Anyone who has that number on their bingo card can cover it with a counter.
The first player to get a horizontal, vertical or diagonal row of four counters wins.

▣ 10, 100 and 1000 bingo

You will need:

- a bingo card
- counters.

1   Take turns to choose a multiple of 1000 and divide it by either 10, 100 or 1000.

For example: $6000 ÷ 1000 = 6$

2   Anyone who has that number on their card can cover it with a counter.
The first player to get a horizontal, vertical or diagonal row of four counters wins.

Mental calculation strategies (× and ÷) 8

You can multiply a number by 9 or 11, by multiplying it by 10 and adding or subtracting the number.

◬ Multiplying by 9 or 11

Work these out by multiplying by 10 and then adding or subtracting.

1   11×11 2 14×11

3   11×16 4 19×11

5   13×9 6 9×17

7   17×9 8 9×18

▣ Multiplying and adjusting

Work out these multiplications by multiplying and adjusting.

1   16×11 2 11×19

3   22×11 4 18×9

5   9×40 6 54×9

Use a similar method for these multiplications.

7   21×8 8 21×14

9   19×9 10 12×19

Mental calculation strategies (× and ÷) 10

You can split numbers into chunks to make multiplying easier.

⚠ 🔁 Empty squares

Solve the puzzle by finding the missing numbers.

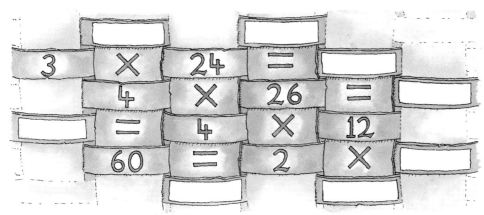

◎ Hidden digits

Find the digits hidden under the stars in each of these number sentences.

1   20 × 3 = ★0

2   4 × 30 = ★★★

3   12 × 4 = 4★

4   23 × 3 = ★★

5   16 × 5 = ★★

🔁 More hidden digits

What digits could be hidden under the stars in this number sentence?
Can you find more than one answer?

2★ × 6 = 1★8

Pencil and paper procedures (× and ÷) 1

You can use doubling and adding to multiply any two numbers.

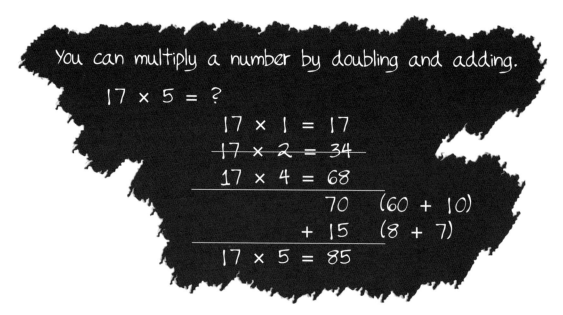

You can multiply a number by doubling and adding.

17 × 5 = ?

17 × 1 = 17
~~17 × 2 = 34~~
17 × 4 = 68
_____
          70   (60 + 10)
        + 15   (8 + 7)
_____
17 × 5 = 85

⚠ ▣ Egyptian multiplication

Work these out by doubling and adding.

1   23 × 7   2   45 × 5

3   36 × 8   4   28 × 6

5   42 × 7

◎ Doubling multiplication

1   23 × 3   2   32 × 5

3   35 × 4   4   35 × 6

5   42 × 3

You can split numbers into chunks to make multiplying easier.

⚠ Marking homework

These are the answers to Saima's homework questions.

Write down an estimate of the answer to each question and then check it. If there is a mistake correct it and then work out the right answer.

1   48 × 6

×	4	8
6	24	48

24 + 48 = 72

2   37 × 5

×	30	7
5	150	35

150 + 35 = 185

3   8 × 64

×	8
6	48
4	32

48 + 32 = 80

4   72 × 7

×	70	2
7	49	14

49 + 14 = 63

5   53 × 5

×	50	3
5	250	15

250 + 15 = 265

6   6 × 45

×	40	5
6	240	30

240 + 30 = 540

➤ Pencil and paper procedures (× and ÷) 2

You can split numbers into chunks to make multiplying easier.

◎ Grid multiplication

Use a grid to help you answer these questions.

1	43 × 3	2	25 × 5
3	32 × 4	4	54 × 5
5	61 × 5	6	28 × 6

▣ Extending the grid

Use a grid to help you answer these questions.
Write down an approximate answer for each question first.

1	78 × 6	2	164 × 3
3	345 × 4	4	208 × 7
5	252 × 8	6	322 × 6

You can split numbers into chunks to make multiplying easier.
There are different ways of recording your working.

⚠ Domino products

You will need some dominoes.

Find different products that can be
made using any three dominoes.

```
    34
×    6
   204
```

◎ More domino products

Use the grid method of multiplication to complete the domino calculations.

1 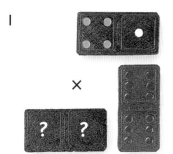   2 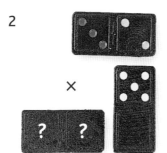   3

▣ Largest products

1   Choose three dominoes. What is the largest
    product that can be made using these dominoes?

2   Choose four dominoes. What is the largest product
    that can be made using these dominoes?

3   Investigate all the different products that can be made
    using three or four dominoes from the dominoes shown.

 ×

Pencil and paper procedures (× and ÷) 5

You can use multiplication to solve some word problems.

△ ◎ ▣ Solving problems

Answer the questions. Compare your methods with a partner.

1   Emma buys three packs of batteries. There are two batteries in each pack. Each battery costs 52p. What is the total cost of the batteries?

2   Some children do a sponsored walk around a running track. Rifat is sponsored for £7 for each lap. She does 23 laps. How much money does she raise?

3   A tin of biscuits contains 26 plain biscuits and eight chocolate ones. How many biscuits are there in the tin?

4   There are three classes in Year 4 at a school. Each class has 29 children. How many children are there in Year 4?

5   Mrs Adelakun buys some paper plates for the school party. She buys 12 packets. Seven packets contain 25 plates. Five packets contain 15 plates. How many plates does she buy?

6   A farmer has 72 eggs. Six eggs fit in a box. How many boxes can be filled?

7   Each section of this CD rack holds 12 CDs. How many CDs does the rack hold?

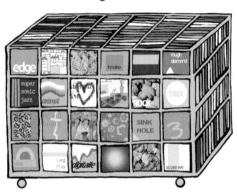

8   A holiday costs £365 for one person for one week. How much will it cost for three people for two weeks?

You can divide by taking away multiples of the divisor.

⚠ ◎ ▣ Digit pairs

0	I	2	3	4	5	6	7	8	9

Choose any two digits that add together to make a number less than or equal to 10.

2 and 6

Use the digits to make two 2-digit numbers.

26 and 62

Add these numbers together.

$$26 + 62 = 88$$

Divide this total by the sum of your two digits.

$$2 + 6 = 8$$
$$88 \div 8 = \boxed{}$$

What do you notice?

You can divide by taking away multiples of the divisor.

⚠ Correcting work

Check if these are right. If they are wrong, show where the mistake is and work out the right answer. If they are right, try to work out the answer in a better way.

1   54 ÷ 6

60 (10 × 6)   −6

0   60

54 ÷ 6 = 11

2   72 ÷ 6

60 (10 × 6)   +6   +6

0   60   66   72

72 ÷ 6 = 12

3   90 ÷ 6

30 (5 × 6)   30 (5 × 6)   30 (5 × 6)

0   30   60   90

90 ÷ 6 = 18

4   84 ÷ 7   84 ÷ 7 = 12

$$
\begin{array}{rl}
84 & \\
-14 & (7 \times 2) \\
\hline
70 & \\
-14 & (7 \times 2) \\
\hline
56 & \\
-14 & (7 \times 2) \\
\hline
42 & \\
-14 & (7 \times 2) \\
\hline
28 & \\
-14 & (7 \times 2) \\
\hline
14 & \\
-14 & (7 \times 2) \\
\hline
0 &
\end{array}
$$

You can divide by taking away multiples of the divisor.

◎ Checking answers

Check if these are right. If they are wrong, show where the mistake is and work out the right answer. If they are right, try to work out the answer in a better way.

1   48 ÷ 3

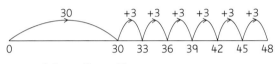

48 ÷ 3 = 7

2   42 ÷ 3

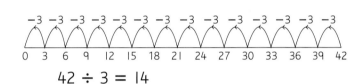

42 ÷ 3 = 14

3   39 ÷ 3

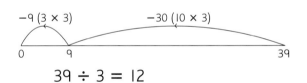

39 ÷ 3 = 12

4   55 ÷ 3

−9 (3 × 3) −3 −3 −3 −3 −3   −30 (10 × 3)

1   10 13 16 19 22 25   55

55 ÷ 3 = 18

▣ Chunking

Write out the answers. Show how you worked them out.

1   92 ÷ 4   2   192 ÷ 6   3   176 ÷ 8

4   140 ÷ 4   5   224 ÷ 7   6   152 ÷ 8

You can use division to solve some word problems.

△ ◎ ▣ **Division problems**

1   An egg box can hold six eggs.
How many boxes are needed for 42 eggs?

2   There are seven players in a netball team.
In a Year 4 class, 28 children want to play netball.
How many teams can be made?

3   A taxi can take up to five people.
38 people need to go to the station.
How many taxis are needed?

4   Some sweets were shared out between 12 children.
They had six sweets each. How many sweets were there altogether?

5   Carol bought four CDs. They were all the same price.
She paid £32. What was the cost of each CD?

6   Dwayne bought five postcards.
They were all the same price.
Dwayne got 5p change from £1.
What was the cost of each postcard?

7   Jez used 102 square tiles to make a
rectangular pattern. There were six rows
in the pattern. How many tiles were
there in each row?

8   Dawn is planting seeds in trays.
She plants eight seeds in each tray.
She planted 96 seeds altogether.
How many trays did she use?

You can use multiplication and division to solve some word problems.

⚠ Word problems

1   A school is planning a trip. The school hires six coaches which they fill. Each coach holds 54 passengers. How many passengers is that altogether?

2   Fireworks are packed into boxes of six. How many boxes of fireworks can be made from 91 fireworks?

3   Josh sells kites. He sells 23 kites at £8 each and two kites at £12 each. How much money does he make?

4   A shop notices that there are 87 shopping days to Christmas. How many weeks is that?

◎ More word problems

1   There are seven days in a week. How many weeks are there in 35 days?

2   A shop sells plants. One plant costs 45p. What is the cost of three plants?

3   Simon has to share 32 pens equally between four tables. How many pens should he give to each table?

4   Five loaves of bread are needed to make sandwiches for a class party. Each loaf costs 39p. What is the cost of the bread?

You can use multiplication and division to solve some word problems.

🔁 Even more word problems

1. A lift can hold seven people. There are 64 people waiting to take the lift from the ground floor to the fifth floor. How many lift journeys are needed?

2. A sports shop sells table tennis balls in boxes of five. There are 115 boxes in the shop. How many table tennis balls are there?

3. Bushes of red roses cost £9 each. Mr Peacock has £120. He wants to buy as many roses as possible. How many bushes can Mr Peacock buy?

4. Meg is going on holiday with her three children.
The cost for Meg is £375.
The cost for each of her children is £190.
What is the total cost of the holiday?

Checking results of calculations 1

You can check the results of addition by adding in reverse order.

⚠ Crystal hunt

The numbers on each planet show the amount of crystals there.

You must:
   begin at START and end at FINISH
   only move up or along
   collect space crystals on the way
   find the journey that collects the most crystals.

➤ Checking results of calculations 1

You can check the results of addition by adding in reverse order

◎ Space hunt

The numbers on each planet show the amount of crystals there.

You must:
- begin at START and end at FINISH
- only move up or along
- collect space crystals on the way
- find the journey that collects the most crystals.

▣ Forbidden planets

The numbers on each planet show the amount of crystals there.

You must:
- begin at START and end at FINISH
- only move up or along
- collect space crystals on the way
- find the journey that collects the most crystals.

Checking results of calculations 2

⚠ Snack shop

1   You want to buy two snacks. Work out the change from £2.50.
    Show how you worked each answer out and checked it.

    a   peanuts and raisins
    b   sesame sticks and cheese dip
    c   cereal bar and peanuts
    d   mini flans and raisins
    e   mini pizzas and cereal bar
    f   raisins and sesame sticks

    e.g. Cheese dip and mini pizza
         80p + £1.00 = £1.80
         £2.50 – £1.80 = 70p
         70p + £1.80 = £2.50

2   Find the totals of these shopping bills. Check by subtracting.

    a   sesame sticks, cereal bar and raisins
    b   mini flans, peanuts and cheese dip
    c   mini pizzas, mini flans and raisins

➤ Checking results of calculations 2

You can check addition by using the inverse operation, subtraction.
You can check subtraction by using the inverse operation, addition.

◎ Fruit and vegetables

Fruit and vegetables

apples, 45p a bag

tomatoes, 50p a bag

cucumber, 65p each

bananas, 80p a bag

cabbage, 75p each

carrots, 35p a bag

1   You have fruit and vegetables to buy. Work out the change from £1 in these problems. Check by adding back. Show how you worked each answer out and checked it.
    a apples, 45p a bag
    b tomatoes, 50p a bag
    c cucumber, 65p each
    d bananas, 80p a bag
    e cabbage, 75p each
    f carrots, 35p a bag

2   Find the totals of these shopping lists. Show how you worked it out and checked by 'taking back'.
    a a bag of apples and a bag of bananas
    b a cabbage and a cucumber

Checking results of calculations 2

You can check addition by using the inverse operation, subtraction.
You can check subtraction by using the inverse operation, addition.

Crisp counter

Crisp counter

salt and vinegar — 75p
Onion rings — 84p
cheese spirals — £1.35
ketchup crunchies — £1.30
CHIPSTICKS — 60p
crispy frazzles — £1.80

1 You want to buy some crisps for a party. Find the totals.
   Show how you worked it out and checked it.
   a two packs of ketchup crunchies and two packs of salt and vinegar crisps
   b two packs of cheese spirals and two packs of onion rings
   c two packs of chipsticks and two packs of salt and vinegar crisps
   d two packs of ketchup crunchies and two packs of crispy frazzles
   e two packs of crispy frazzles and two packs of onion rings

2 Calculate the change from £10 for each set of shopping.
   Show how you worked it out and check your results.

Checking results of calculations 3

You can check halving by doubling and doubling by halving.

Write about the strategies you use on RS 161.

△ Book sale

1   Work out how much each book will cost if it is half price in the sale.
    Check your results by doubling. Show how you worked it out.

2   If these are the sale prices, work out what the real price is.
    Show how you would check your answer.

◎ Toy sale

1   Work out how much each toy will cost if it is half this price in the sale.
    Check your results by doubling. Show how you worked it out.

2   If these are the sale prices, work out what the real price is.
    Show how you would check your results.

Checking results of calculations 3

You can check halving by doubling and doubling by halving.

🔲 Sports sale

1   Work out how much each sports item will cost if it is half this price in the sale.
    Show how you worked it out and check your results.

2   If these are the sale prices, work out what the real price is.
    Show how you would check your results.

Checking results of calculations 4

You can check multiplication by doing the calculation a different way.

△ Playing time

1

Activity	Time spent every day
a	playtime	20 minutes
b	football before school	15 minutes
c	lunchtime club	25 minutes
d	register task	18 minutes
e	writing	35 minutes
f	eating lunch	12 minutes

Elaine does these things every day at school.
How many minutes does she spend on each activity in a week?
Show how you checked each answer.

2   a Elaine spends 50 minutes in a week on handwriting. She has two lessons of equal length per week. How long is a handwriting lesson?

b She spends 120 minutes on PE. She has four lessons of equal length each week. How long is a PE lesson? Show how you can check your results.

You can check multiplication by doing the calculation a different way.

◎ How much time?

1

Activity	Time spent every day
a milk	10 minutes
b changing for PE	6 minutes
c reading	15 minutes
d filling in homework diary	12 minutes
e assembly	20 minutes
f maths challenge	8 minutes

These are activities that John does every day at school.
He does them all five times a week.
How many minutes does he spend on each activity in a week?
Show how you worked it out and how you checked each answer.

2   In a different school, children spend this amount of time on different activities in a week.

a Silent reading   50 minutes
b Drinking milk   25 minutes
c Assembly   100 minutes

How much time do they spend on each activity in a day?
Show how you worked it out and how you checked your answer.

➤ Checking results of calculations 4

You can check multiplication by doing the calculation a different way.

▣ Time to spare

Activity	Time spent every day
watching television before school	10 minutes
helping with washing up after breakfast	10 minutes
helping with washing up after tea	15 minutes
homework	35 minutes
playing football	12 minutes
playing games on the computer	18 minutes
watching television after school	28 minutes

Tariq does these things every school day.
How much time does he spend in a week on these activities:

a watching television

b washing up

c homework

d playing games inside or outside?

Show your working and your checking.

2 a He visits a friend for 45 minutes four times a week.
How long does he spend with the friend each week?
Show your working and checking.

b He walks to school three days a week. It takes him 23 minutes.
How much time does he spend walking to school?

You can check calculations by rounding the numbers to the nearest 10 or the nearest 100.

Approximate first

You will need RS 164.

Calculate

+20

+8

43

63

71

Use the grid on RS 164 to record your answers.

1   39 + 42

2   161 + 37

3   48 − 23

4   121 + 32

5   117 − 19

6   148 − 27

7   102 − 58

8   152 + 112

9   97 + 29

10   210 − 42

▣ Approximate to calculate

You will need RS 164.

Use the grid on RS 164 to record your answers.

1   369 + 124

2   272 + 137

3   481 − 128

4   293 − 132

5   134 − 21

6   21 × 9

7   51 × 4

8   122 × 4

9   235 − 98

10   36 × 5

Checking results of calculations 6

You can use what you know about adding and subtracting odd and even numbers to help you check your calculations.

⚠ Let's investigate

Investigate these three statements. Are they true or false? Show how you decided.

1   The sum of two even numbers is odd.

2   The sum of two odd numbers is even.

3   The sum of an odd and an even number is odd.

4   The sum of three odd numbers is even.

5   The sum of three even numbers is even.

◎ What will it be?

121	239	168	137
312	182	45	264
101	94	110	83

Choose a number. Show what kind of numbers add up to make this number.
Are they both odd, both even or odd and even? Try this with different numbers.

► Checking results of calculations 6

You can use what you know about adding and subtracting odd and even numbers to help you check your calculations.

⌨ A different investigation

Investigate these three statements. Are they true or false? Show how you decided.

1   The difference between two even numbers is odd.

2   The difference between two odd numbers is odd.

3   The difference between an odd and an even number is odd.

4   The sum of three odd numbers can never end with the digit 0.

5   The sum of three even numbers can never end with the digit 2.

Solving problems 3

You can write money amounts in pence, or pounds and pence, and easily change from one to the other.

 ## How much money?

You will need:
- a group of four players
- sets of money cards cut from RS 169.

Game rules

- Deal four cards to each player.
- Each player makes the smallest amount of money they can using three of their cards.
  They record the amount in pence and in pounds and pence.
  The player with the lowest amount scores 2 points.
- Now each player makes the largest amount they can using three of their cards and records it in pence and in pounds and pence.
  The player with the highest amount scores 2 points.
- Each player finds the total of their highest and lowest amounts.
  The players with the largest and smallest overall each score 2 points.
- Each player finds the difference between their highest and lowest amounts.
  The players with the largest and smallest difference each score 2 points.
- The winner is the player with the highest score.
- Play the game again. Who is the winner after six rounds?

You can solve a problem by deciding on the calculation that is needed.

⚠ Problem bank

1 Chris buys a pack of 48 stamps to add to his collection of 126 stamps.
   How many stamps has he now?

2 Yusaf had 93 football cards, but he lost 15 on his way home. He then gave 20 to his
   brother. How many did he have left?

3 It takes Martin eight seconds to write his name.
   How long would it take him to write it six times?

4 Sara shares her pack of 60 toffees equally with two friends.
   How many do Sara and each friend get?

5 Naomi puts four cherries on each of the
   12 buns she has made.
   How many cherries does she need?

6 Doughnuts are sold in packs of eight. How many
   packs can be made from 100 doughnuts?

You can solve a problem by deciding on the calculation that is needed.

7

Three children measure their
shadows. Claire's measures 135 cm,
Fiona's is 144 cm and Harry's is 161 cm.
What is the combined length of their shadows?

8 Kate buys a pack of 200 stickers.
She gives 24 to her friend and ten to her brother.
How many does Kate have left?

9 There are 90 children at the Saturday club.
They form teams of six players each.
How many teams will there be?

10 Ali cuts 35 cm from a piece of ribbon 189 cm long.
How much is left?

11 My Dad watches the news at 6 o'clock.
The programme is 30 minutes long.
How much time does he spend watching the
news in one week?

12 There are 36 counters in a pot.
Each child takes four counters.
How many children can do this before all the counters are taken?

Solving problems 7

You can solve a problem by deciding on the calculation that is needed.

◎ Word problems

1   You have 33 monster cards.
    You win 27 more.
    How many have you now?

2   Sam gets a bag of cherries.
    There are 43 cherries in it.
    He gives 15 to his brother.
    How many does Sam have left?

3   Yasmin wants to give five stickers to each of
    her six friends. How many stickers will she need?

4   Pete has 36 sweets.
    He shares them with Gary and Jermaine.
    How many sweets do they each get?

5   There are three seats in a fun boat. How many
    children can go in seven fun boats?

6   A gardener planted 26 tulips, 38 irises
    and 14 daffodils in her garden.
    How many plants were there altogether?

➤ Solving problems 7

You can solve a problem by deciding on the calculation that is needed.

7   You find 24 conkers on Monday,
    31 on Tuesday and 44 on Wednesday.
    What is your total?

8   Liam has 68 Smarties and wants to
    save 24 for tomorrow.
    How many can he eat today?

9   The Nature Show television programme
    is 55 minutes long.
    Jill has been watching it for 16 minutes.
    How much longer will the programme last?

10 Paula ties four streamers to each balloon.
    How many streamers will she need for nine balloons?

11 Aisha counted minibeasts.
    She found 13 millipedes, 39 woodlice, 27 aphids and six spiders.
    How many minibeasts did she find?

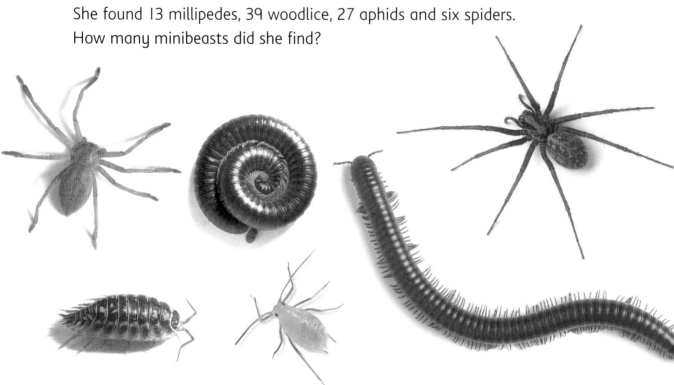

ou can solve a problem by deciding on the calculation that is needed.

Problem calculations

1   Jo is given 17 badges to go
    with her collection of 55.
    How many more will she
    need to make her total 100?

2   A balloon seller started the
    day with 75 balloons.
    She sold 23 in the morning, 36 in
    the afternoon and 16 before she
    went home. How many balloons
    did she have left at the end of
    the day?

3   Mrs Green gives three dog biscuits to
    each of her three dogs every day.
    How many dog biscuits will she use
    in one week?

4   a Kate buys a pack of 200 stickers.
       She gives 27 to her friend and 12
       to her brother.
       How many are now in the pack?
    b She wants to keep 100 for herself.
       How many more can she give away?

5   A recipe tells you to put six olives on a mini pizza.
    A jar contains 45 olives.
    Will you have enough olives to make eight mini pizzas?

You can solve a problem by deciding on the calculation that is needed.

6 a At the funfair, the River Ride boats hold six people.
      How many boats will a group of 39 children need?
   b Are all the boats full?

7 There are three programmes I wish to see. They last 35 minutes, 45 minutes and
   1 hour 15 minutes. How much time will I spend watching them in total?

8 You decide to share a pack of
   100 sweets with the other 29 children
   in your class. How many sweets will
   be left over if you share them
   fairly?

9 a Mrs Gyimah has a box of 200 crayons.
      How many children can each take eight crayons?
   b Will there be any left over?

10 In a pool, there are 39 golden carp, 47 silver carp and 19 koi carp.
    If the pool should only hold 100 fish, how many should be removed?

11 An electrician cuts a 15 m length of cable from a 100 m roll.
    The next day, he cuts a piece which is twice as long.
    How much is left on the roll?

12 Shaynee runs for 10 minutes every morning
    and 20 minutes every evening. How many hours
    does she spend running in the month of June?

30 days hath
September, April, June
and November ...

Solving problems 9

You can check your answer using the inverse operation.

⚠ Check with the inverse

You will need RS 185.

Work out the answers to the problems below, filling in the steps on the solving grid. For each answer, write a number statement using the inverse operation. Use this to check your answer.

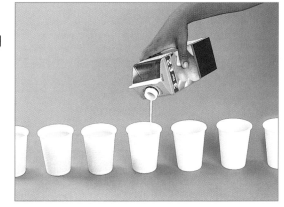

1   How many 125 ml cups of orange
    juice can I pour from a 1 litre carton?

2   A CD rack holds 180 CDs.
    There are 37 empty spaces.
    How many CDs are in the rack?

3   Elli is counting her badges. She has
    14 animal badges, 33 badges from places
    she has visited and 28 advertising badges.
    How many badges does she have altogether?

4   Jodi puts 36 jelly tots on top of a cake.
    How many jelly tots will she need to decorate
    five cakes?

5   You walk 1.3 km to school every day.
    How far will you have walked in one week?

6   Rob saves 15p every day during June.
    Will he save enough to buy a book costing £4.99?

*30 days hath
September, April, June
and November ...*

➤ Solving problems 9

You can check your answer using the inverse operation.

▣ Check, check, check

You will need RS 185.

Work out the answers to the problems below, filling in the steps on the solving grid.
For each answer, write a number statement using the inverse operation.
Use this to check your answer.

1 How many pieces of ribbon 60 cm long can be cut from a 3 m length?

2 Asif wants to try to swim a total of 10 km in one week. On Monday he swims 1.9 km on Tuesday 2.2 km and on Wednesday 0.9 km. How far has he left to swim?

3 Crisps are sold in multipacks containing six bags.
   There are 29 children in Mrs Datar's class. She wants to give a bag of crisps to each child. How many multipacks does she need?

4 There were 254 children at a school. One summer, 31 left and 27 new children joined How many were then in the school?

5 How many days are there altogether in April, May, June and July?

6 Sacks of sand weigh 35 kg.
   Tim says that 25 of them would
   weigh 1 tonne. Is he right?

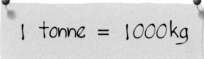
1 tonne = 1000 kg

7 Stamps are sold in books of 12.
   How much will a book of 35p stamps cost?

ou can find rules which explain the patterns you find when you investigate hapes.

⚠ Borders around borders

ou will need square coloured tiles.

1   Make this shape using square tiles of the same colour.

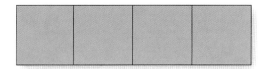

2   Use another colour of tile to make a border all round this shape.
    How many tiles did you need?

3   Continue to make a border for each new shape, working out how many tiles you need
    for each border. Use a different colour for each border.

4   Organise your findings in a table.
    a Can you see a pattern?
    b Explain how the numbers for the borders are increasing each time.

Challenge
Explain why the numbers increase in this way.

You can find rules which explain the patterns you find when you investigate shapes.

▣ More borders

You will need square coloured tiles.

1   Make this shape using square tiles of the same colour.

2   Use another colour of tile to make a border all round this shape.
    How many tiles did you need?

3   Continue to make borders. How many tiles do you need for each border?
    Use a different colour for each border.

4   Organise your findings in a table.
    a Can you see a pattern?
    b Explain how the numbers for the borders are increasing.
    c Why do the numbers increase in this way?

5   Work out the patterns for these shapes. How does each pattern grow?

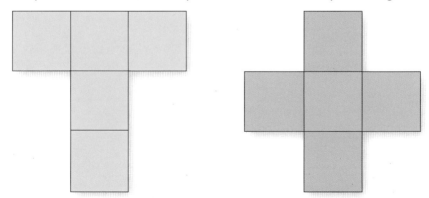